Aug 99

To David
with all my
Best Wishes
Shalom

Laura Varon

THE JUDERIA

Laura Varon. Copyright: Nick Del Calzo

THE JUDERIA

A Holocaust Survivor's Tribute
to the Jewish Community of Rhodes

Laura Varon

PRAEGER

Westport, Connecticut
London

Library of Congress Cataloging-in-Publication Data

Varon, Laura, 1926–
    The Juderia : a Holocaust survivor's tribute to the Jewish
community of Rhodes / Laura Varon.
      p. cm.
    Includes bibliographical references and index.
    ISBN 0–275–96346–2 (alk. paper)
    1. Varon, Laura, 1926– . 2. Jews—Greece—Rhodes (Island)—
Biography. 3. Holocaust, Jewish (1939–1945)—Greece—Rhodes
(Island)—Personal narratives. 4. Rhodes (Greece : Island)—
Biography. I. Title.
    DS135.G72R489 1999
    949.5'87—dc21   98–36733

British Library Cataloguing in Publication Data is available.

Library of Congress Catalog Card Number: 98–36733
ISBN: 0–275–96346–2

First published in 1999

Praeger Publishers, 88 Post Road West, Westport, CT 06881
An imprint of Greenwood Publishing Group, Inc.

Printed in the United States of America

The paper used in this book complies with the
Permanent Paper Standard issued by the National
Information Standards Organization (Z39.48–1984).

10 9 8 7 6 5 4 3 2 1

*This book is dedicated
to my two grandchildren,
Lior and Maya Dahan
from Rehovot, Israël.
And to my two daughters,
Clara, who always
encouraged me to write
my story, and Renée, who
is a passionate reader.*

In memory of . . .

My Grandmother Rachel Cohen

My Mother Reina Cohen Varon

My Father Salomon Varon

My Aunt Diana Cohen Hasson

My Uncle Shumuel Hasson

My little Cousins Jaco and Matti Hasson

My Aunt Fortune Cohen

My Cousin Moise Varon

My Friend Lucia Modiano

My Friend Matilda Israel

My Friend Marie Binun

My Friend Jaco Halfon

My Friend Salvo Cohen

My Friend Peppo Hanan

My Friend Perla Hasson

. . . and to all the "Others."

CONTENTS

ACKNOWLEDGMENTS

IF IT WASN'T for Sharon Gricol, my memoirs would have never been written. If it was not for Roger Hoffman, my story would have never been written so beautifully. To Heather R. Staines, Ph.D., my editor, thanks for believing in my story from the beginning and thanks to everyone at Greenwood. I would like to express all my gratitude to Uncle Nissim Cohen from Cape Town, South Africa. To Maruska, wherever you may be, the Russian political prisoner who taught me how to survive Birkenau, and to Laura Codron from Stockholm, Sweden, for keeping me awake in Bergen-Belsen at the very end just before the liberators opened the door, I am eternally grateful. To Norman Kunkel, who participated with the British in the liberation of Bergen-Belsen, and his wife Georgia Kunkel. In meeting Mick Garrett, along with his wife, Tasha, we found a common bond, as he is writing his own story and helped me with my publishing questions. To Marilyn Parsons, my good neighbor of many years, and to my soul sister, Brenda Inman, thanks for your friendship. To Kay Greenberg, the teacher who encouraged me to write my story; to Pedro Velez, former journalist at American Field service; to Kate Greenberg, who, during the service of Bat Mitzvah, remembered the young girls of the Holocaust who never had the chance; to Joel Hoffman who, during the service of Bar Mitzvah, remembered the young boys of the Holocaust who never had the chance; to Mary C. Hertel, a Woodinville High School student, for her beautiful poem, "Born"; to Grace Hofrichter, a Woodinville High School teacher and to all the teachers and students around the Seattle and Tacoma areas; to all the girls at Northgate Domus; to Paule J. Thornton; to the University librarian, Kaisa London, for her help and encouragement; to Mr. Benton Arnovitz from the Washington Holocaust Museum for all the information about publishers; to Nomi Halpern and Braha Rivline from Yad Vashem Holocaust Memorial in Jerusalem, Israel; to Stella and Renée Levi (survivors); and to my daughters, Clara and Renée— thank you very much.

1.

JOY

IN THE SPRING OF 1938, I was twelve years old and lived with my family along the narrow streets behind the walls of the Citadel of Rhodes. Our house was near the center of an area in the Citadel called the "Juderia," and all around us it seemed that the streets and buildings were filled with laughter, happy conversation, and the sweet sounds of Orthodox ritual. My father, Salomon, used to say, "Del Dio y del visino no se puede enkuvrir, porke primero vemos la kara del Dio y despues la del visinio": You cannot keep a secret from God, nor from your neighbor—because after God, your neighbor is the first one you encounter in the morning. He was right, of course, because we lived shoulder to shoulder with our relatives and neighbors, packed tightly within the confines of the mile or so that encompassed our community.

But we never felt crowded. We never felt confined by the width of the narrow streets. You see, each of us was bound together by our traditions, and we were linked irrevocably to the beauty of life in this beautiful place called Rhodes.

We lived simply in those days. For the most part, our homes and businesses consisted of one- and two-story block buildings of hewn stone, most constructed in the Middle Ages. In the Juderia, the elegant or striking architecture one might expect of an ancient city was replaced by practical, flat-roofed buildings, seemingly squeezed into every inch of space within the Citadel. Though the casual observer might think the gray and tan walls of the Juderia uninspiring, they encompassed the most beautiful places I have ever seen.

We walked where the ancient Greek poets and philosophers

walked. We lived among the constructs of Roman and Genoese sea-
farers and merchants. We felt protected by the Citadel walls, built
before the Crusades by the Knights of St. John. And everywhere, we
could touch their lives. Whether carvings or statues or the old, hand-
hewn walls of the buildings themselves, the evidence of centuries of
habitation were all around us, and the ghosts of the ancients seemed
to guide our care of their city. Some said that the first inhabitants of
Rhodes were descended from Helios, the Greek god of the sun, and
the nymph Rhodon. Others believed that Rodanim, a direct descen-
dant of Noah, was the first man on the island, arriving during the
second generation after the Great Flood. But it really didn't matter
what one believed. We Jews were a part of Rhodes's history. We had
lived on Rhodes at least since the days the Torah was first written.
As we had been throughout the world, we were also the caretakers
of others histories. The Juderia was a clean place, nearly unchanged
since the Middle Ages. We kept it that way because it was beautiful
and suited our lifestyles, yes, but also because of our inherent, abid-
ing respect for those who had come before us.

My family lived on the ground floor of a two-story house on Via
dei Ricchi, a few twists and turns from the Kahal Gadol synagogue
and La Kay Ancha, the wide market street that was the center of our
commerce. My father had come to Rhodes from Turkey several years
before when his family home had been burned out during an upris-
ing. My mother's family had been in Rhodes since the time of the
Inquisition. Her ancestors had been among the Jews forced to leave
Spain by Ferdinand and Isabella. Faced with the prospect of death
or forced baptism, they fled east to Rhodes, then a part of the Ottoman Empire. Wisely, Bayezid II, the Turkish Sultan, foresaw that
Spain's Jewish expulsion would be the empire's gain. He recognized
the talent, culture, and tax revenues that the Jews would bring. He
encouraged the exiles, my mother's family among them, to resettle
within his Ottoman realm. Coincidentally, my father's forebears had
settled in Turkey proper as a result of the same invitation. Mother
used to quip that surely the two families were on the same ship from
Spain. After getting to know my father's ancestors, hers quickly departed the ship in Rhodes!

My mother, Regina, was a serene, beautiful woman. We children
were instinctively drawn to her because her calm, rational sense
seemed to us like an island in the midst of Father's fiery sea. She
nurtured each of us differently, in a way that made us feel at times

that each of us was her only child. Mother represented security, common sense, and that innate knowledge that within her consistency and purpose we could always find quiet contentment.

Father, too, provided us a sense of security, but far differently than did Mother. His arms were like our own private Citadel, surrounding us in the knowledge that he would readily defend his family from any threat. His eyes would sparkle with pride at the slightest accomplishment on our part, but that sparkle could change to a raging fire upon transgression—either from one of us or, particularly, from someone outside the family. I loved him so. As a child and a young adult, I always knew where I stood with Father, and I always knew that his love for us was far deeper than any he could convey. How many times I came home to hear his boisterous melodies. How many times I would walk through the door only to see him bound down the stairs, singing one of the old songs, that wonderful sparkle in his eyes.

Uncle Nissim has told me many times that of the four children, I am the most like Father. He says that Father carried the fires of Spain in his heart and that I carry that same flame. "A flame born in the old days of the Inquisition," he says. "A proud, ethical drive to defend and protect one's own." Perhaps, but I still wonder if my survival over the years was the result of Father's gift, fate, or just the whim of chance.

Mother and Father made sure we carefully observed the rituals of our faith and the customs of our community. Our lives revolved around our Jewish heritage, and our special days, such as Purim, Passover, and the High Holy Days, were always met with extensive preparation and sincere observance. I can still remember the Succah we built in our little courtyard for the celebration of *Succot*. Father constructed it meticulously, and we adorned it with palm branches and myrtle. How the sweet smell of the leaves mingled with aromas of blossoming orange trees or the grape vines that found toeholds in the cracks of the house walls. We would pray and study the *tikkun* beneath that simple splendor, ensconced in our observance and surrounded by Mother's *biscochos* (cookies) and fruit we had hung on the Succah branches.

Father's many tales were a special source of happiness for all of us. As long as we could remember, Saturday evening after *Havdallah* had been filled with tales of Djoha, Ginha, or any of several other folk characters from our Turkish and Spanish traditions. And while many of father's stories would simply invoke laughter, Saturday evening tales always seemed to be chosen for their moral, for the life's lesson they might impart. These were the stories I loved most. I knew I would lie snugly in bed this night, thinking of father's story until my brother Asher's steady breathing led me to drift into sleep.

Father sat in his accustomed chair by the charcoaler. The little creaking stove took the chill off Rhodes' cool evenings, and had always been our gathering place for stories and long conversations. Having finished my after-dinner tasks quickly, I sat cross-legged on the floor between father and the charcoaler, followed shortly by my younger brother Asher.

"Do you have a story, Father?"

"Perhaps I should tell you the story of Laura. Not our Laura, no, but like her, a young, beautiful woman."

I blushed, but relished the attention.

"The Laura of this story was beautiful, but lonely. And one day, she sat crying beneath an Amora tree. It was a warm, wonderful summer day, but Laura cried and cried. Her father and mother were loving parents to her, but Laura cried."

Father paused, rolling the ash off his cigarette and into an ashtray.

"Along the road nearby came a wise man. He was very old. He was so old that his beard reached almost to his feet. He was so old that his walk was barely a shuffle. But he had the wisdom of all his many years, and he noticed the beautiful Laura crying by the Amora tree."

Father took on the character, speaking in a small, crackling voice.

" 'Why do you cry so, little one?' he asked. Laura told the old wise man that she dreamed that someday a young man as fine looking as a prince would come and, with much love for her, take her away from the simple life she had with her family. She was crying, she said, because she wished so much that day were here today.

"The wise man leaned forward on the cane he carried to help his walk. 'You are a young and beautiful woman,' he said. 'But you do not yet know what there is to know. Be careful of your wish, for it may come true.' "

Father leaned back in his chair, again taking a puff on his cigarette.

"And time did pass, and as fate would be fate, the beautiful Laura met and fell in love with a fine young man who was intelligent, wealthy, and handsome. They married, and soon he took her far away from her home, far away to a place of great majesty, with wonderful, friendly people."

I caught Father's eye. He smiled a wry smile as he spoke. From my cross-legged perspective, it was as if he were telling the tale only to me.

"And time passed, and as fate would be fate, Laura sat beneath a huge, ancient tree. The tree was very beautiful, with long, drooping branches full of leaves and flowers that perfumed the air all around. But the tree seemed somehow sad, and beneath its sad, drooping branches Laura cried like before. And do you know? Along the road near the tree came a very, very old wise man. He was so very, very old that his beard dragged on the ground behind him as he walked."

Father stood up momentarily, stooping over as if to imitate the wise man's walk.

"He was so very, very old that each step he took was very, very slow."

Asher laughed at Father's gestures.

"But being a very, very wise man," Father continued, "he recognized the beautiful Laura from beneath the Amora tree of years before. He slowly, very slowly, came to her, and leaning on his cane, eyed her with a knowing smile.

" 'Why do you cry?' he asked. 'Is it because your dream of long ago came true?'

"And the beautiful Laura nodded. She told the wise man how she had met and married the handsome young man, and how he had taken her to the beautiful land. But she longed so for her home. She missed her simple life, and that was why she cried."

Father now leaned forward, looking carefully at each of us as he spoke.

"And the wise old man said: 'Never forget from where you came, or you can never know the direction you are going. Do not try to live in the past or in the future, but never forget from where you came, or you can never learn to be happy today.' "

"So what happened to Laura, Father?" It was Stella, her face a little blush from her close proximity to the charcoaler. She was our youngest, and I sometimes resented the attention Father seemed to pour on her. Still, in those days Stella and I were close. I suppose her quiet demeanor reminded me of Mother, and I think Stella found safety of sorts in my Father-like nature.

Father held out his hands plaintively. "We'll never know for sure Stella, but we can hope she heeded the wise man's advice, and learned to be happy with all that she had, learned to remember her past without wanting to live in it.

"The lesson of the story, children, is to remember. Remember the good things you did, and learn from the mistakes you made in the past."

Mother entered the room. "Come little ones. Time for bed."

One by one, Stella, Joseph, Asher and I each hugged Father good-night. As his arms encircled me, I gazed over his shoulder at a picture of my great-grandmother Strea. She stood in the photograph, stern and taught and embroiled in Sephardic orthodoxy. But she always seemed to speak to me, especially on Saturday nights. It was as if she somehow knew me, could look right through me from that picture, could speak to me across whatever boundary separated this existence from hers. "Remember your beginnings, Laura. Remember that your beginnings are today."

I closed my eyes as Father kissed my cheek.

At the time, I had no idea how much my father's story that night would shape the rest of my life. For as he was fond of saying, "fate would be fate," and there would be many times that I would find it necessary to remember my past as a means, literally, of staying alive. There would be many times and places in which I would need to close my eyes and find great-grandmother Strea, and try again to make her speak to me.

But for now, I knew nothing of such troubles. Life in the Juderia was filled with the simple pleasures of family and neighbors, and the exuberance of my youth. Our community seethed with the rigors of day-to-day life, and the smells of the bakers and orange trees, and the sounds of song and laughter.

For most of the community, the Sephardic customs, traditions, and superstitions that had evolved over the centuries were embraced as a fundamental part of our everyday lives. Within the warm cloak of this heritage, I knew a simple contentment and security. The tenets of tradition were seldom questioned, for life was good.

Together with the celebration of Shabbat, Jewish holy days were a cornerstone of this tradition. Their coming was cause for solemn preparation and ritual throughout the Juderia. In joyous holy days, particularly Purim, their observance in Rhodes was marked with exuberant celebration.

For me, the first day of the festival of Purim had been filled with excitement. As was our custom, my sister Stella and I had spent nearly all morning traversing the Juderia, accepting gifts of money from family and relatives. Dressed in costumes of Queen Esther that Mother had laboriously sewn, the two of us had visited the home of every aunt and uncle we could remember. Uncle Rahamin had given us both a princely sum, commenting dutifully on how grand our costumes were. Grandmama, plying Stella and me with *desayuno de keso* (cheese pastrie), had filled our purses with a handful of coins. It was more money than I ever had in one place at one time. As the two of us now arrived home for the *Sueda de Purim* meal, the stuffed purses bounced heavily against our thighs with a satisfying chunk-chunk-chunk as we walked. I could barely contain my anticipation and excitement. Tonight there would be music and dancing at the Purim street fair in La Kay Ancha (The Wide Street). Tonight my friends and I would wander among the booths for hours, playing games for prizes, eating sweets and candies, singing songs. And from now until late afternoon, Stella and I and our brothers would join a throng of family to tell stories, sing songs of Purim, and eat, and eat, and eat. As the two of us approached the door, we were greeted by our mother and the delicious smells of broiled meats and other foods near-ready for the meal.

Mother had filled the table so full that the entire surface was covered. The table seemed an overloaded testimony to the bounty of life on Rhodes. In addition to Uncle Rahamin's *palamida*, there was *kapama*, a baked fish dish made with chopped tomatoes, onions, green peppers, and parsley; *tomat*, preserved green tomatoes; broiled beef patties, freshly baked coarse bread and rolls; and a variety of appetizers and side dishes prepared by my aunts. For the adults, the meal was accompanied by *raki* (a liquor that had given the men a jolly glow since early afternoon). And after the meal, when cigarette and pipe smoke mingled with the smells of food and the charcoaler, there would come another wave of delicacies: roasted watermelon seeds, roasted chick peas, white raisins, and Grandmama's sponge cake.

Mother welcomed the walk to La Kay Ancha after the Purim meal. It was a simple way to ease the overstuffed feeling she and everyone in the household seemed to have after such largess. We would stroll through the little streets as a group, the women engaged in happy conversations with the children or each other, the men boisterously waving to neighbors they passed, belching occasionally from the mix of too much food and a little too much *raki*. For Mother, it was an endeavor each year, a specific objective, to recreate these happy moments with family through preparation of a repast fit for royalty. It was a matter of tradition, a matter of personal pride to at least match those special Purims she'd known as a youngster. And so it was for every mother in the Juderia.

I remember how the heavy, sweet smells of the house gave way to the fresh air of early evening Rhodes as we began our stroll. The streets were already filled with other families, embroiled in merriment and animated conversation as sunset embraced dusk. *La Kay Ancha* was only a half a mile or so away, and I could hear the faint sounds of music mingled with the greetings of neighbors and the laughter of our lighthearted crowd.

The reassuring *chunk chunk* of my purse promised me more happiness to come. Soon there would be games to be played. Soon there would be sweet treats to be purchased from the many carnival vendors. Soon there would be dancing late into the night. For now, my sister and I danced about the family group, injecting bits of young anticipation into the smiling little throng.

Every side street to La Kay Ancha spilled out hundreds of people into the broad street that marked the center of old Rhodes. Carnival booths and vendor stalls, most of them manned by Greeks, lined the Way. Little bands of musicians were everywhere, each with its group of dancers from the crowd. Some of them made fair attempts at playing and singing the more modern music of the day, and others played the traditional songs with eloquence and expertise. For some reason, I seemed to prefer the traditional music. Having been given my freedom to roam the area free of the family, I found myself with a dozen others listening to a small band at one end of the Way.

There was a special magic to Purim, and especially to the Purim carnival. For as long as I could remember, I would always find myself with the friend or friends I wanted to be with the most, despite the two thousand people wandering about *La Kay Ancha*. I could remember wanting to dance with Jaco, and we would somehow find each other in the crowd. "This is a magical night," I thought to myself. I closed my eyes and let the strains of the music soothe me. I inhaled deeply, and the smells of Greek and Sephardic cooking seemed to combine in the fresh air to form a sweet, heady fragrance.

That night, we wandered the course of La Kay Ancha many times, guided by an invisible network of relatives who somehow managed to keep track of us. We danced with our friends Jaco and Salvo, and even Uncle Rahamin. We ate candies and baked treats we bought from the Greeks with my midday treasure. I treated my school friend Lucia to *sumada*, thick, milkshake-like drinks flavored with cinnamon that seemed only available during Purim. The two of us played many games of chance, vying intently for the small prizes offered by the carnival vendors. We had our fortunes told and our palms read, and we danced many more times with our friends.

I could feel a sense of contentment as if it were tangible. It wrapped around me like a protective coat, surrounding me in the warmth generated by my own happiness. For tonight at least, companionship and contentment walked hand in hand around La Kay Ancha. I knew this feeling from many past Purims. I just didn't know what to call the feeling except happiness.

The road near the village of Trianda is lined with fig trees, and among them stands an Amora. In the early mornings of spring, before the breeze comes in off the Aegean, the Amora turns the still air syrupy with the vanilla-like scent of its flowers. And this spring morning, Uncle Rahamin, Jaco, Salvo and I sat quietly at its base, recovering from the efforts of the bicycle ride up from Rhodes.

For a time no one spoke, preferring instead to listen to the quiet of a still-sleeping countryside, and luxuriate in the Amora's heady perfume. Perhaps I savored the moment the most of the group, for as its youngest member my opportunities for these adventures away from home had been few.

Even though life in the Juderia seemed to continue as it always had, 1938 brought with it a strange foreboding, an odd undercurrent of insecurity, even for me. I'd heard the tense conversations of my father, mother, and grandparents about the rumors of new racial laws aimed at the Jews. I'd heard the talk that the governor might soon close the Collegio Rabbinico, the local Sephardim's proud institution of higher education. Still, such troubles seemed of little consequence, especially under the peaceful arms of the Amora tree.

Prejudice among the many peoples on Rhodes ebbed and flowed like the tide. It was as much a product of the close-knit communities on the island, like the Juderia, as it was an accompaniment to the superstitions bred through centuries of cultural ignorance. Rhodes had always been a crossroads for a wide variety of peoples, many of whom came there because they had been displaced by religious or political persecution in their homelands. And they brought with them a strong adherence to the traditions and customs they had known in their countries of origin, and the people of the Juderia were no exception. For the most part, religious and cultural tolerance was the norm among the Greeks, Jews, Turks, and often gypsies on the island. But there were frequent exceptions to the rule, generated by ignorance or superstition on both sides of the cultural fence. Depending on the government in power when such exceptions occurred, the superstitions could compound into a relatively large-scale persecution of at least one of the peoples involved. Over the years, that had most frequently been the Jews.

For me, prejudice was an uncomfortable new concept. That my occasional spats with the Greek children were sometimes carried on by adults but on a much larger scale made me uneasy. I was certainly old enough to recognize the value of friendship and tolerance, regardless of the beliefs of my counterparts. It was difficult for me to believe that friendship could be undermined by ignorance, yet I reluctantly accepted the fact that it sometimes was, and even that *my* lack of understanding could, on occasion, be the cause.

But I shrugged off such uncomfortable thoughts and feelings quickly. My view of the world, though narrowed by life on Rhodes, was by and large an optimistic one. I tended to look for the best in people first and was generally tolerant of those personal traits I either didn't understand or didn't agree with. If I had a fault, Mother would say, it was that I was too trusting of what I believed to be the positive motives in everyone. Father worried that my naiveté would get me into situations I didn't yet understand. Unfortunately, he was right.

In the summer, the gypsies would appear on Rhodes, setting up large camps in and around the Citadel. As was their custom, they came to trade with the people of the island and to sell trinkets and fortunes and stories of far-away places they had been. To the people of Rhodes, there was a strange attraction about them, but one that was tempered by superstition. The gypsy camp was not a place I should have been. Every summer, my parents had dutifully warned me that the area where the gypsies were was strictly off-limits.

Nonetheless, one summer afternoon I found myself walking with my friend Lucia in the area just outside the Citadel. As was our habit on many warm afternoons, we would take long, conversation-filled walks about the city, exploring again what we already knew.

Years later, I would not be able to recall what our conversation had been about, only that it was an intense discussion. And as such intense dialogues between adolescent girls go, we paid little attention to where we walked. All at once, it seemed, we looked up to find ourselves but several yards from the edge of the gypsy camp.

Lucia, her dark hair framing the sudden fear in her eyes, immediately began to turn away, almost in a bolt. But I quickly grabbed at her arm.

"Wait, wait, Lucia."

"We need to leave, Laura. Right now!" Lucia was intense with her fear.

"No. Wait. It's all right. Look."

I pointed toward one of the gypsy tents, just a little to the right of where we stood. An elderly looking woman, dressed in the colorful garb of the gypsies, stood waving to us. I was not too far away to see the smile on her face, a genuine look of warmth that quickly dispelled what little fear I had.

"The woman there. Do you see?"

"We're not supposed to be here, Laura. Let's go."

I looked at Lucia dubiously. "Let's see what she wants, Lucia. Look, she's an old woman. She won't harm us."

The woman continued to motion for us to come forward. Her smiling, unspoken invitation was too much for me to resist. I began walking toward her, pulling the still-fearful Lucia along.

"God told me last night I would see you," the woman said, "and that I should tell your fortune."

The two of us looked at each other. "But we have no money."

The woman continued smiling. "It is God's wish that I tell your fortune. There is no cost to satisfy an old woman's charge from above."

Lucia was afraid to look in the fortune-teller's eyes. She stood slightly behind me, staring down shyly. "Which of us did God tell you to seek?"

"The one with little fear."

Lucia breathed a perceptible sigh of relief. She and I had always joked about my sense of adventure and Lucia's sense of reserve. We had no doubt who should have her fortune told.

"Come. It is God's will."

As I cautiously walked toward the woman's tent, I whispered to Lucia to stand close by the door and to run quickly for help if anything strange occurred. The fortune-teller, still smiling, seemed as if she had overheard my order.

"Don't worry. Your friend will be safe here."

The inside of the tent was dim, save for the small light provided by a few candles. Its coolness struck me, as did the strange smells of smoke and incense. There was little in the way of furnishings. A

small table and chairs stood in the center of the space. As she removed her scarf, the fortune-teller motioned me to sit in one of the
chairs. She disappeared for a moment into an adjoining room, reappearing with a deck of cards. She sat at the table across from me and,
still smiling, began to slowly shuffle them.

I guessed the fortune-teller was only a little younger than Grandmama. She was very slim, with long, straight hair and a dark olive
complexion. Her face seemed a good face, one that I could trust. But
her eyes were very dark and mysterious. They seemed to be a strange
life force that glowed from a face creased and wrinkled by the hard
gypsy life. But I was captivated by her smile.

The woman placed the cards on the table carefully and began
turning them over one by one. I watched her expression as she manipulated the cards, and her smile slowly faded. She suddenly closed
her eyes, as if in some sort of self-induced trance.

"What is it?"

The fortune-teller motioned a pause with her hand. I sat in silence
for several minutes, watching the woman's quiet trance.

I began to feel insecure. I thought momentarily of running from
the tent, but Lucia's occasional noises just outside helped me calm
myself. Besides, I thought, the fortune had yet to be told.

The woman opened her eyes slowly, and I leaned forward in cau-
tious anticipation. But the fortune-teller no longer smiled. She
sighed, looking down again at the cards she had turned. She looked
away from me, seeming to stare off into another place.

"I see uniforms in your cards."

"Uniforms? What sort of uniforms?"

"I cannot tell. Strange uniforms. Strange colors I have never seen."
The woman rubbed her chin, shaking her head slowly. "I believe
they are soldier's uniforms, but I do not know what country they are
from."

I fidgeted uncomfortably. It was as much the woman's sudden worried demeanor as it was the message of the uniforms. "I . . . I should
go now."

As I began to leave the tent, the woman touched my arm. I turned,
and without a word we embraced. Though every instinct told me to
run away, the touch of the woman was both calming and reassuring.
She stood back a half-step, still holding my shoulders in her hands.

"There will be a time when you are in great danger, little one.
That is why the cards worry me so. You will know danger well. You

will know it so well that you may take its presence for granted. Beware of this, child. Beware the danger the uniforms bring."

She again embraced me, whispering in my ear. "But do not fear the uniforms. Fear knowing danger too well. Beware that danger may grasp you when you think you know it will not. Go with God."

I shivered, and swallowed hard. I said nothing, but squeezed the woman's hand as I turned away.

I couldn't understand the significance of the woman's prophecy or how uniforms might play a role in my life. I quickly shook off the foreboding she had given me and discarded her words as just so much silliness. Still, as Lucia and I walked toward home, we spoke quietly about the strange meeting with the fortune-teller. I made her promise not to tell of our encounter, particularly not to our parents. Lucia quickly agreed, extracting the same promise from me. She knew the trouble she would have been in even for standing outside the woman's tent. Dealings with the gypsies should be left to the adults, and, in retrospect, we understood why. We had such limited perspective on life that we had no way of putting the gypsies' prophecies and superstitions into any sort of logical context. With sudden pangs of guilt for our transgression, we resolved never to enter the gypsy camp again.

Of course, I never spoke of the incident with anyone beside Lucia. Still, I quietly questioned what the fortune had meant. I looked at anyone in a uniform differently now, wondering to myself what effect the soldier or officer I faced might have on me. And though I rationalized away her words, I would never forget that day in the tent. In later years, in fact, I would remember her prophecy vividly.

2.

WAR

THE YEAR 1939 was a year of massive change, little of it for good. With Hitler's advance on Poland, war in Europe escalated rapidly, and its effects were felt throughout the Mediterranean, even on Rhodes. Some of those impacts at first seemed unimportant to the people of the Juderia, like the replacement of Governor Mario Lago with de Vecchi. But in a relatively short time, life on Rhodes changed from simple, rustic splendor to an oppressive quiet.

It became apparent to all of us that there were now no guarantees of our safety. Those subtle changes on Rhodes came with an ominous correlation to past persecution of Jews everywhere, but the community generally discounted any similarities with history. We preferred to ignore and retreat from conversations that made uncomfortable references to the beginnings of bigotry. "Rhodes is too small," the rabbis would say. "We are too insignificant for the world to worry about." As a result of our cowering acceptance, the subtle alterations to the fabric of life on Rhodes imposed by the government were quietly incorporated into the tapestry of the Juderia.

But the tapestry was becoming frayed, and it happened over the course of only a few months.

By the beginning of 1939, even I had papers identifying me as a Jew. I had to carry them everywhere, but "everywhere" was now limited to certain parts of the city and certain times of the day. Everyone in the Juderia was now restricted. Shops we had once frequented were now off-limits to us. The parks could be visited only at certain times. And because shipping in the Mediterranean was now a dangerous endeavor, the supplies of imported staples Rhodes had come to depend on had begun to dwindle.

While the Italian army had always maintained an unobtrusive presence on the island, that presence was now bolstered by the fascist dictator directing it and by the onerous presence of the new governor. Soldiers seemed to be everywhere. What had once been part of the "decor" of the Rhodes tapestry now clashed with the life of the Juderia in every respect. Intercultural friendships, such as those enjoyed between our family and many Greeks, were now strained and difficult. The instinctive fears and superstitions held for centuries were now harsh, conscious realities, even though no one seemed to know quite what to fear.

Every person on Rhodes reacted differently to the changes brought by the fascists. Some accepted them and adjusted their actions accordingly; some rejected them with dangerous acts of compassion. There were several shopkeepers who, having had long-standing relationships with the people of the Juderia, now quietly let them enter their stores to obtain goods and precious foodstuffs. That such activities put the shopkeepers in danger of arrest was of little consequence, for the value of humanness far outweighed the worthlessness of directed hate.

On the other hand, many of the Greeks seemed to embrace the newly sanctioned hatred for us. To me, they seemed to be caught up in it as I had been so often caught up in the community's celebration of Purim. Instead of joy and sharing, however, the subject of this celebration was intolerance.

The school we attended was forced to close, and we were redirected to the Italian Catholic school in the newer part of Rhodes. It was here that I first noticed the strange contrast between my life and the lives of my non-Jewish counterparts. I had become fearful and reticent, spending most of my free time at school in the library. I would spend many hours there, quietly staring out the window at the Italian schoolgirls playing in the courtyard, as they always had. Their lives seemed full of the youthful exuberance and everyday conversations that were now so foreign to me, for my life had become full of whispers—ominous whispers of persecution and torment, like an unending dark mist that weighed down the spirit. I and many of my friends had become so fearful that we dared not think of the cause of the fear.

In a strange way, the pervasive foreboding that flooded the Juderia bred hope. Few people would accept, much less even think about, the fact that persecution was now rearing its head all around them. Few gave credence to the idea that their hardships were merely the tip of a horrible iceberg. Things just had to get better. Surely, I thought, this was still a new century and a new age. It was inconceivable that people could be as barbaric as they had been in the past.

At least at home I could find escape from this strange depression and fear. I busied myself these days helping Mother and my sister prepare Auntie Fortune's trousseau, and it was a task that was full of romantic ideals and hope. Despite the difficulties in traveling anywhere, we all still clung to the belief that Auntie Fortune would soon leave for the Belgian Congo. And what for her was a carefully planned reality was for me a source for fantasies of adventure and romance. In that quiet world between awareness and sleep, I would find myself in Auntie Fortune's place, feeling the steamy heat of an imaginary jungle, protected by the strong arms of the man I loved.

But oppression, fear, and uncertainty swallowed all of us. Among the anti-Jewish laws that the governor had passed was one stating that all Jews who had arrived in Rhodes after 1919 would be deported. This affected almost a third of us, my father included. For months, we lived in horrible uncertainty, not knowing how we would leave, how we would afford the trip, or where we would go. But thanks to the intervention of Jewish organizations in England and France, Mussolini later agreed that the Jews in question could not be expelled because their Italian citizenship had been granted through the Treaty of Lausanne. Unfortunately, Governor de Vecchi only stated that the local law would be suspended. He did not tell us when or if it would be rescinded, so our fear continued unabated.

Father finally made plans to leave, regardless of the legal outcome. He had learned of a ship that was going to stop in Rhodes, and he had decided that we would leave aboard it for Palestine. By the time the ship arrived, we had packed enough of our belongings for an extended trip. The house would be left with its furnishings. Father kept telling us that this would be a temporary relocation. "Perhaps a few months," he had said, "until Rhodes is again safe for us."

But it was not to be. The morning after we had packed, Grandmama arrived at the house in tears. She pleaded with Father not to leave. Rhodes was home, she begged, and Rhodes was the only home she knew. If the family left, she would remain with no one. She could not bear to leave the home her forebears had made since the thirteenth century. She pleaded with Father not to take her daughter and grandchildren away.

Reluctantly, Father conceded to her wishes. Although fearful for the safety of his family, he still held a belief that Rhodes was too far away and much too small for Hitler to be interested in. A mere handful of Jews surely would escape notice. As such, Grandmama's protestations to him were enough to tip the scale. With some apology, he told us to unpack. It was a decision made by emotional commitment, and similar ones throughout the Juderia sealed the fate of many that day. At the time, no one knew that there would be no more opportunities to escape. There would only be three more ships.

I was relieved. Despite the oppressive place that Rhodes had become, home was still home, and the old, narrow streets of the Juderia were still warmed by the sun, still filled with the footsteps of history I so loved.

I was even more relieved when I discovered what had happened to the ship. It had stopped in Rhodes, bearing about 600 Jewish refugees from eastern Europe. Many from the Juderia joined them, and the ship set sail after a very brief stay in port. But after only several hours of steaming, a fire broke out, and the old ship limped into the island of Samos. From there, everyone was brought back to Rhodes in small boats, most with nothing more than the clothes they were wearing. Sadly, those from the Juderia returned to their homes instantly destitute. As for the European Jews, they stayed outdoors in the stadium where Lucia and I had met the gypsy fortune-teller.

I suppose that hardship has a way of bringing out the best in people. It certainly did in us. For despite our difficulties, in spite of our fears, we in the Juderia took blankets and food and warm clothes to the Jews in the stadium that day. None of us, save perhaps the rabbis, had ever seen hassidim, those strange-looking people with their black hats and odd, curled hair. But like us, they were Jews. And they, like Jews everywhere, were in trouble. For a few precious days in the spring of 1939, many of us gave them almost everything we had. We fed them. We clothed them. Most frightening of all, we talked with them.

Father had always seemed so strong to me, but that night when he came back from the stadium, I saw fear in his eyes for the first time. It was more than the uncertainty I had sensed previously from both Mother and him. It was that hollow, nervous stare that belied more than foreboding.

We young people were never told what Father had heard, but it likely concerned the terrors just beginning then in Europe. Jews, after all, were disappearing by the trainload, and the laws we suffered with under Governor de Vecchi were nothing compared to what had prompted that shipload of humanity to leave everything for a chance aboard a rusting ship to Palestine. But that night, I remember hearing the muffled sounds of Father and Mother talking in their bedroom. There was somehow something different about those sounds, though to this day I cannot tell what. Perhaps it was just that they continued long into the darkness.

By a miracle, our community leaders managed to find another, smaller ship to take the stadium Jews to Palestine. Within a few days they were gone, but we were not among them. Perhaps we would be ignored, like the few bees that survive the bear's destruction of the hive.

Despite the pall of uncertainty that had settled over Rhodes, we found ways to continue our lives and our customs. The old synagogues were still the center of the community, and the rabbis still managed to ensure the orderly observance of tradition. It was, after all, so fundamental to all of us, so enmeshed with life itself, that our Judaism could not be thought of as a religion, or at least not in the sense of the Christian view of observance. In the Juderia, keeping kosher and keeping tradition was not something one did because the rabbi expected it. It was not something one did for fear of condemnation. It was, simply, a part of each and every one of us, an ancient core of what we were as individuals and as a community. As much as anywhere else in the world at the time, Judaism on Rhodes was a culture, one that was steeped in the traditions and ancestry of its practitioners. Though rigid and constraining from an observer's perspective, Judaism provided a secure, nearly inpenetrable framework within which intellectualism had flourished for thousands of years.

One had to be Jewish to understand, to even begin to comprehend what being a part of the culture really meant. For while the infusion of a Jewish presence in dozens of other communities throughout the world had often resulted in economic prosperity and significant intellectual benefits, those solid bulwarks of Jewish tradition and observance formed a wall that both protected and separated the Jews from the communities they lived in. Unfortunately, that separatism, particularly when combined with the general happiness and emotional well-being typical of the Jewish community, often fostered insecurity, jealousy, and contempt by non-Jews. What was now beginning to creep into Rhodes was only the latest chapter in a centuries-old book of intolerance and hatred. Most of those chapters had been started when the Christian or Arab ran up against that wall of tradition and observance. The chapter had been completed when resulting insecurities about the Jews were brought to the boiling point by religious demagoguery concerning the Jews and Christ, by political fervor over rights to property, and as recently, by dictators intent on finding an easy scapegoat for economic woes.

While I understood little of this, I felt all of it. What had been an innocent, rustic life for me behind those walls of tradition had now become clouded with fear and whispers. Still, I managed to cope. There were brief moments of sunshine in the gray, brief moments when my friends and I managed to part the clouds with imagination and, for us, daring.

Despite his father's objections, Uncle Nissim's son Moise had elected to stay in Rhodes. Although Moise was barely 19, he had a good job and a girlfriend whose family had no intention of leaving. In the months after Uncle Nissim had departed for Palestine, Moise found himself spending increasingly more of his spare time with our family. We were, after all, now the closest thing he had to family of his own. Despite the fact that the mail was inconsistent at best, Father and Moise often exchanged bits of information they had each received in sporadic letters from Uncle Nissim.

As had become his habit, Moise arrived at our house early Saturday to celebrate Shabbat with the rest of his "new family." As was our custom, we had been in synagogue all morning and had returned home for the midday meal, to be followed by a walk to the village of Rhodino.

Because I was only one year younger than Moise, we instinctively found many areas of common interest and many subjects for animated conversation. During the family's walks on Shabbat afternoons, he and I often walked a distance ahead or behind the main family group, oblivious to their pace due to our topic of discussion at the moment. It seemed that I could talk with Moise about nearly anything, and our conversations were always easy and lighthearted.

We certainly would have discussed the onerous depression we both felt most of the time, but the topic was typically avoided. The reason was simple: Both Moise and I found our walking talks on Shabbat a small escape from the drudgery and fear we usually felt. For us, discussing such things would have been a travesty against this small bit of comfort, this small piece of togetherness, we both felt. Saturday walks were something we quickly looked forward to.

One Shabbat afternoon, Moise and I were, as usual, walking a good distance in front of the family group. After several shouted requests that we wait for the rest to catch up, Father, at my insistence, gave his permission for us to go ahead on our own. Within a half-hour, we found ourselves at the small cafe on the outskirts of Rhodino. It was a place I knew well, for I had come here with the family many times to enjoy the food and the scenery. Though it was small, the village was famous locally for its peacocks that seemed to wander every-where. But they particularly seemed to favor a magnificent sculptured garden that adjoined the cafe. Here, amid the wonderful smells of food and the quiet bustle of the cafe, one could sit overlooking the garden and gaze for hours on these magnificent birds among resplen-dent, lush flowers and foliage. I always seemed to become entranced in this place. I could sit for hours without a word, staring off into the beauty of the garden, letting its delicate smells and colors take me away from the grays of my life. Moise, a slender young man with dark, curly hair and brown eyes, took advantage of my quiet medi-tation to catch his breath from our fast walk.

Despite Father's trust in Moise's behavior and observance of cus-tom, I knew he had a mischievous streak. Today was no different. As I sat still staring off into the garden, Moise gently touched my elbow, startling me. He smiled a little smile that belied the twinkle in his eyes and called the waiter.

"Would you bring us some bread, salami, and a little wine?"

The waiter nodded quickly and turned away. I sat transfixed now by Moise's order. My eyes were as big as saucers, and he laughed aloud at my obvious surprise.

"What's the matter, cousin?"

I was nearly speechless. "But, but . . ."

Moise shrugged. "I know, I know. It's not kosher." He leaned forward a little. "But Laura, why shouldn't we live a little in times like this? Why shouldn't we enjoy life when we can?"

My surprise quickly turned to laughter. My immediate fear at disobeying custom was rapidly replaced by a sincere pleasure in Moise's little trick. That Father was so trusting of him made me laugh even harder. I realized that Moise had just done what was probably the only thing he could think of to bring a little humor into what had become a rather dark and depressing existence. To be caught by Father, after all, was a wonderful fear to have, for it replaced the greater, sinister fears that surrounded us all, even for only a few moments.

Moise stuffed a piece of bread into his mouth. "Well?" he mumbled, pointing at the salami.

Instead, I reached for my glass of wine, tipping it slightly, as if in a toast, before sipping. "Moise," I laughed, "you are a good friend, and an even better cousin."

The two of us laughed and talked for a half-hour or so until we thought the rest of the family would arrive in the village. At Moise's suggestion, we ran down the tiny street to a medieval fountain, where we hurriedly washed and drank away our misdeed. But I would long savor my first taste of the vine and the sweet flavor of the salami. It had been a moment when darkness gave way to sunshine, however brief. I would remember its warmth for many years.

But these few years had not been kind to anyone in the Juderia. For most of us, the oppression and fear brought on by the government's new policies were bad enough; the progressive lack of food was an ominous sign of things to come. Within months of our visit to the cafe, such luxuries as salami could only be had from the black market at great expense. For most, our family included, the daily diet now consisted primarily of white cabbage and, at times, a little coarse dark bread. Despite our collective insistence on tradition, everyone was getting thin. There was simply not enough food grown on the island to support its population. Since the port had been closed to all commercial traffic since that last ship left, foodstuffs had become progressively scarce. Compounding the problem, the limitations on shopping placed on the people of the Juderia made their general condition far worse than most of the island's inhabitants.

Beginning in 1942 with sporadic warnings, air raids on Rhodes had become a consistent, destructive reminder of the state of the world around us, and the Juderia was very close to the port. The planes would always come at night, and roused by the sirens from our sleep, we would race the mile or so to the air raid shelter, waiting out the heavy "whump, whump, whump" of the bombs.

I detested the raids, but not out of fear of destruction. I had become thin and quiet, undernourished by my continuous cabbage diet, and these days I looked forward to sleep as perhaps the ultimate escape from fear. That I should be roused from that sleep, that I should have even that peace taken away from me, made me angry. As much out of some unspoken defiance as out of modesty, I insisted on completely dressing—undergarments and all—before fleeing to the safety of the shelter. Father would repeatedly scold me, sometimes heatedly, but it made little difference. It was my way of insisting on some sort of civility amid all the madness.

Still, life struggled on in the Juderia, almost in spite of itself. While the bombs fell at night, I spent as much time with my friends as possible by day. I still took an occasional walk with my friend Lucia Modiano, and we still wondered aloud about the gypsy woman's fortune. I would spend considerable time with Peppo Hannan, a high-school soccer player with a sizable crush on me. I would ride my bicycle with Jaco and Salvo when I could, and I once thought of taking a chance by riding out to the Amora tree. But most of all, I spent time with Nino.

I had met Nino, strangely enough, through Peppo and his friendships with the local Italian air force contingent. But while Peppo had a romantic interest in me, I was entranced with Nino. And perhaps Nino represented the first inkling of the danger the gypsy woman had foretold. I couldn't tell whether it was his piercing blue eyes, his uniform, or his quiet, confident manner that made me feel so wonderful and simultaneously unsure of myself. But Nino was like an emotional whirlpool. I wanted very much to be in its center with him, to feel these strange new emotions and sensations that coursed through me whenever I was near him. It was just that I wasn't sure I'd survive. There was danger here, yes, and an enticing warmth I had never known before.

It was so strange, I'd tell Lucia. We seldom spoke much, and our time together was limited because of his military duties. But I instinctively knew that Nino felt as much emotion as I did. I could see it in those deep, gentle eyes, and I could instantly sense it in the touch of his hand.

Nino was in his early twenties, and after a short time he got to know where we lived. He walked past our house every morning on his way to the Italian headquarters nearby. I always waited expectantly and bounded down to the courtyard to sit with him. We talked, but not too much. For the most part, we simply sat close to one another, holding hands and communicating in ways only the innocent at heart can. For the first time, Nature's quiet voice had spoken to me. I answered by reveling in the soft warmth of Nino's confidence.

And all at once, he was gone. There were no good-byes between us, but despite my sudden sense of loss, I somehow knew there didn't need to be. For a few weeks that spring, young love had taken me far away from the depression and fear I lived with daily. For a few precious moments, I had been spared the misery of reality. And I had learned the pointlessness of yearning for what I couldn't have. If there was no bread to go with the cabbage, there was simply no bread. Wishing there was, was an exercise in futility. If Nino was not here, I could not bring him back by wishing it so. However brief, I was simply grateful and deeply touched by the journey we had shared.

Strange incongruities seemed to permeate every aspect of life in the Juderia those days, and those caught up in them were enmeshed in a dawn-to-dark rush between contentment and despair. By day, I had wistfully gazed upon the face of love, while by night I struggled to get dressed before the bombs fell. Only a year before, Father would have harshly discouraged my relationship with Nino. Today, he simply said nothing, hoping vainly that if the worst did come, at least I might be spared for the sake of a "friendship." In the mornings, the rabbis and scholars in the Juderia would have long intellectual discussions on topics ranging from religion to science. By the afternoon, they stood in line with everyone else, looking hopefully for an extra bit of bread or, if they could afford it, perhaps a piece of cheese. In the summer of 1943, my Auntie Diana had become pregnant with her second child. By that fall, Hitler would control the island.

Like everything else in Rhodes those days, it all happened so strangely. With Italy herself being invaded, war had not been going well for Mussolini, and the armistice between Italy and the Allies was being negotiated. Believing that the Dodecanese Islands were strategically important, with Rhodes as the chief island in that group,

Churchill directed an attempt to negotiate surrender of the islands with the local Italian garrison.

On the night of September 9, 1943, Major Earl Jellicoe, an interpreter, and a signalman parachuted onto Rhodes. Jellicoe carried with him a personal letter to Admiral Campioni, the Italian commandant of the island, from Britain's Sir Henry Maitland Wilson, Commander in Chief of the Middle East. Unfortunately, their landing did not go well. The three of them were separated and the interpreter was injured. When the local troops found Jellicoe, he destroyed the letter by eating it, and the interpreter could do nothing to explain their presence on the island without the proof provided by that letter. For his part, Admiral Campioni was unsure of the support the British would provide if he complied with the armistice. The 7,000 German troops who arrived on the island a few days later sealed the fate of the inhabitants. Campioni surrendered to the Nazis.

At first, things went a little better on Kos and Leros, the islands nearest Rhodes. The British sent a battalion of soldiers to bolster the Italian garrisons on both islands and, with Allied air support, held control for a time. But more pressing tactical needs on the Italian mainland drew the planes there, and the Germans counterattacked with a vengeance. Within days, nearly 12,000 British and Italian troops were captured on Kos and Leros, and the entire Dodecanese area was under full German control.

In the Juderia, we still struggled to live normally, but the struggle by now was extremely difficult. In January 1944, Auntie Diana gave birth to Matilda, and on the Shabbat following the birth, the family had carefully prepared a complete celebration of the little girl's naming, as was the custom. The rabbi would come to properly name the baby, and relatives and friends from throughout the Juderia would attend. Grandmama played a large role in the preparation, doing much of the baking and cooking herself. Uncle Rahamin and Auntie Fortune lived with her, and the three of them had pooled their limited money for months to purchase the necessary goods on the black market.

I had a special relationship with Auntie Diana, and the birth of little Matilda was an event greeted with much anticipation and joy. For years, I had gone upstairs every Friday afternoon to watch little Jaco, Diana's first-born, while my aunt bathed for Shabbat. After the bath, I would tend Diana's long, light-brown hair, brushing it carefully and setting it into the styles Diana preferred. It was a part of weekly life I particularly loved. We would have long conversations while I brushed her hair, and we would share intimacies as if we were sisters.

And this Friday night was the most special of all. Diana and Uncle Shumuel's flat was spotless, having been readied for the baby-naming the next day. Grandmama and Uncle Rahamin were there, too. He helped out where he could while Grandmama busily prepared baklava and other sweets for the celebration. To this day I don't know how Grandmama managed to procure such rarities as sugar for her baking, but it was almost as if things had somehow, magically, returned normal. There were smiles and happy conversations all around me as the work went on. Uncle Shumuel carefully and constantly tended to little Matilda while Diana bathed, his pride and happiness beaming from a constant grin. Uncle Rahamin whistled a familiar song as he worked, and the sweet smells of Grandmama's baking permeated the house. I was most conscientious tending to Diana's hair. Using a pearl-studded comb, I carefully fixed her hair in a stylish but conservative fashion, all the while sharing the excitement of tomorrow's event through animated conversation.

When I finished, Diana took a hand mirror to examine my handiwork. She said nothing, but I knew she approved from the smile on her face. Auntie Diana had often complimented my efforts, saying I had a special talent with hair. But tonight, as I finally found my way downstairs, I knew I had done an exceptional job. Even Father noticed my obvious pride as I walked in the door. Sitting in his chair by the charcoaler, he smiled a broad smile at my beaming face.

Even though celebrating the birth of a girl, according to tradition, was nowhere near as formal as that provided for boys, Matilda's naming was nonetheless a most special event, especially with the difficulties of everyday life. It was more than just an escape from the frightening presence of the German military. It was a quiet statement of defiance, a quiet refusal to succumb to the torment, ridicule, and persecutions imposed by our new "benefactors." A quiet demonstration that, in spite of the inhumanities and cruelty being imposed by the "modern" world, what we were and what we would always be lived on. Regardless of the uncertainties of the near future, today was a clear reminder of our roots. It was something that no one, not even Hitler himself, could wrest from me or any of those around me.

In the morning, Uncle Shumuel attended synagogue, and during the course of services was serenaded by the entire congregation with special songs asking God's blessing on the new child. In the afternoon, many friends and relatives appeared in Diana and Shumuel's home, singing more songs and bringing small traditional gifts for the baby. The service itself was brief. The rabbi, dressed in special robes for the occasion, chanted a song of naming to Diana and Shumuel, holding little Matilda. As was our tradition, she was formally named after Uncle Shumuel's mother.

What a strange, eerie world of contrast and contradiction life had become for us. On the one hand, people struggled to persevere in their traditions and way of life. On the other, the oppressive presence of the Germans might as well have changed that beautiful blue Dodecanese sky a pallid shade of gray. Everywhere, the outward signs of life's hardships were becoming more and more apparent. Staples, especially items like sugar, virtually disappeared from the shelves of even non-Jewish vendors and were so expensive on the black market as to be beyond the reach of even the wealthy. Everyone seemed listless, going about their daily chores and rituals as much by habit as by any sense of desire. And most of all, the signs of war began to appear with disturbing regularity.

Whether by intent or by casualty of the bombings, the air raid warning system under the Germans was not nearly as reliable as it had been in 1942. Sometimes, the sirens sounded only moments before the bombs fell. Sometimes, the only warning the people of the Juderia had was the sudden explosions in and near the harbor. Sometimes, the bombs missed their targets, and people and property became innocent victims.

By the spring of 1944, Hitler's fortunes were changing. The Allies had landed in Europe, and after the hard winter in the east, Russia had just begun taking back her territory. In the Mediterranean, Germany's air power had dwindled, and with what little resources they had were now called to defend Europe and the east. As a result, Allied bombings of Rhodes no longer took place only at night. Now the bombers came by day, too, and with the little warning provided by the Germans, the people of the Juderia were constantly at risk.

On the first day of Passover, Father was in the synagogue, and Mother and the rest of us had just finished preparing for the midday meal. My brothers and I were outside, and I sat beneath the orange tree in the courtyard. It was in full bloom, and its flowers filled the air with a wonderful sugary scent that made me think of better times.

My brothers, Asher and Joseph, were nearby, playing a game I don't remember.

There were no sirens this time, no sudden explosions. But as I sat watching my brothers, a faint, familiar sound came to me. I instinctively looked up through the branches of the orange tree and saw a glint of silver high in the sky. As the sound became louder, I sat transfixed. There were so many tiny shapes in the sky, and against its blue, they looked like some strange confetti drifting through the still morning air.

Mother rushed out of the house, "Laura! Asher!" The droning sound of the aircraft was now replaced by the screaming whistles of falling bombs. "All of you!" she screamed as the first explosions threw me to the ground. "Inside, inside now!"

The strings of bomb exploded across the harbor in quick, deafening blasts. In La Kay Ancha, the old marketplace where I had spent so many Purims, two little boys raced across the open street. In a shuddering blast, they simply disappeared, replaced by a huge crater in the middle of the marketplace.

Mother huddled us all in a corner of the living room. She cowered over us, her grasp becoming tighter with each blast. The house shook violently, and we were all at once covered with dust and shards of glass that flew everywhere as the windows blew in. Asher screamed at first, but mother held us all tightly to her. She began softly, her words drowned out by each blast, then louder as her voice came back to her from the terror we all felt.

"*Shema, Israel. Adonai Eloheinu, Adonai Echad*"—Hear O Israel. The Lord our God, the Lord is One.

And as quickly as it had all begun, the blasts stopped, followed by a frightening silence. There were none of the sounds we had come to take for granted. There was no noise from the street and no longer any sound from the sky. There was nothing, save the shivering sound of our breathing.

None of us moved. After a moment, Mother began repeating the *Shema* over and over again.

I peered over Mother's shoulder out into the house. The table we had so carefully set for the midday meal was now overturned against the charcoaler. Glass from the broken windows lay everywhere, mingling with shards of pottery from the dishes that had been blown off the table. The tablecloth lay in a disheveled heap across Father's chair, which had somehow remained in its place. Everywhere, what had moments before been at least a physical representation of our lives was now a broken, shattered remnant.

I stood up and cautiously walked across the room. Carefully, I picked up Great-grandmama Strea's picture from the floor and replaced it on the wall. She gazed at me through the cracked glass of her picture frame.

"Regina? Asher?" The sound came to my ears full of fear.

"It's Salomon! Come on. Let's get up now!" Mother stood carefully, helping each still-shaking child to his or her feet.

"Father! We are here!"

He burst through the door, shoving it open as he pushed away debris. At the sight of us, he stopped suddenly.

"We are all right, Papa. All of us are all right."

Father clasped his hands together. At the first sounds of the bombs, most of the congregation in the synagogue had crouched between the pews amid screams of terror. But Father's first thought was of his family. He had raced out of the synagogue just in time to be thrown violently to the ground by the concussion from a bomb that fell in the marketplace. He had run through the streets, somehow avoiding flying glass and debris amid the falling bombs, and he now stood before us, only minutes after the last explosions. Tears streamed down his cheeks, making little rivulets across his blackened face. His arm had been cut by flying debris and was bleeding noticeably, but he didn't seem to care at all. He just stood there, weeping without sobbing, staring with a combination of relief and unbelievable sadness at what had become of our world.

He wiped his cheek, smearing the soot and dust and tears. "Thank God all of you are all right." He held Mother in an embrace that was somehow different from any I had ever seen. "We must leave the Juderia. The planes could come back soon."

"Where will we go, Papa?"

"I think we should try Izguro. I know some people there, some Turkish. I think we can find a place there." He paused. "I want you to all find clothing for a few days and bring it with you. We will pack as fast as we can and leave today."

When we left the house, it was as if we stepped into another world. Our little courtyard seemed embraced in the deepest winter, for all the blossoms and leaves of the trees had been blown to the ground. The bomb that blew out the windows had detonated less than a hundred feet from our house, and across the street, what had once been a doctor's home was a pile of rubble. I could see the smoke from fires here and there, and everywhere, it seemed, people were fearfully calling out for their relatives. In La Kay Ancha, the spot where Lucia and I had had our wonderful evening at the Purim carnival now no longer existed. There was only a huge pile of broken rubble and wood to mark the place, adjacent to a huge crater where the two little boys had vaporized.

No one said a word. We just walked along the tiny streets, enmeshed in our own thoughts that embodied a strange mixture of loss and relief. For a while, thankfully, we were all still alive and together; what had been an idyllic home and world for us was now irrevocably changed. I knew it would never be the same again.

When the bombs fell that day, twenty-six people lost their lives in the Juderia, and many more were injured. Among them, Cousin Moise, caught too close to a bomb blast, had lost his leg. He would spend the rest of our time in Rhodes in the hospital. Though I didn't know it at the time, our visit to the cafe would be the last time I would ever speak with him.

By nightfall, we began to settle into a small house in Izguro. Through Father's contacts and good fortune, he had indeed been able to rent the place from a Turkish family. It was small, consisting of little more than a downstairs living area and a loft above. We decided that Salomon and the boys would sleep downstairs, while Mother and I shared the loft. When we left the Juderia, Grandmama, Auntie Diana, and Uncle Shumuel had also looked for a place to rent, and they had found one in the village of Candilli. With Uncle Rahamin, Auntie Fortune, my sister Stella, and the other children, they managed to crowd into a home somewhat larger than the one Father had found. For her part, Stella had wanted to remain with Grandmama, and Father knew she would be safe with them in Candilli. And for the next few months, Father walked 45 minutes to get to work each day and returned home at night with whatever belongings from the Juderia we needed. So, too, my brothers and I walked to school each day via the same route. We would wait for Stella along a path that led the three or so miles between Candilli and Izguro.

That path led through a rather large woods and past hundreds of bivouacked troops, both German and Italian, that were stationed all around the villages. Despite my fear of them, I would often travel the distance between our new home and Grandmama's to visit Stella or, as I was fond of doing, spend time with Auntie Diana and the children.

If it was available, Auntie Diana would always make me fried egg-plant and, if they were lucky enough to have it, spread a little yogurt over the dish. We would lay out a blanket and eat outside in the sunshine; Auntie Diana, little Jaco, baby Matilda, and me. The farm-like setting reminded me of peaceful Rhodino and the Amora tree and of those happier times I'd spent with Jaco, Salvo, and Uncle Rahamin. I would sit back and bask in the sunlight and enjoy the gentle wisps of perfumed air that came off the land. And I would marvel at little Jaco, who understood nothing of the reasons for his new home, but who delighted in the everyday discoveries he'd make in his new surroundings.

But wherever we went, it somehow seemed like the pincers of oppression were closing in on us. Troops were everywhere these days, and the bombings would at times come dangerously close to the villages. Even that gentle path between Izguro and Candilli be-came a dangerous thoroughfare.

As I approached the woods one day, I was stopped by an Italian soldier who, after examining my papers, asked me why I was going off into the forest. I told him, of course, that I was walking to Candilli to visit my aunt.

But the soldier told me not to go through the woods. They had been mined, he said, and a few little boys had even been killed while playing there.

I wasn't afraid of the mines, and I wasn't afraid of the soldier. But I could feel myself flushing red with anger. How much danger, abuse, and inconvenience did the innocent have to take? How long would they all have to live like sheep at the hands of the wolves? I turned away from the soldier and began walking down the path, into the woods, as I always had.

"Did you hear what I said? Are you crazy?"

I waved him off, without looking back to see if he was chasing me. I just kept walking, at a brisk pace, down that path and directly into the mined forest. At that moment, I didn't care if my legs were blown off or even if I died from stepping on a mine. I was just angry. Angry at the soldier for taking away my pathway. Angry at the Germans for sapping my strength and spirit. Angry at the world for taking away these months and years, for slowly destroying the lifestyle of inno-cence we loved so much.

I threw myself to the ground with the first explosion. As had been my habit. I had gotten out of bed, put on my underwear and clothes, shoes and coat, and then walked toward the shelter as the air raid sirens wailed. But tonight the bombs were falling too fast for my time-consuming habit, and I had only been a few yards out the door when the first explosions rumbled near Izguro. Just as suddenly, the Italian and German antiaircraft batteries began firing, shaking me violently.

The noise of the explosions and the guns was so extreme that I suddenly could no longer hear them. I could only feel the ground shake beneath me and the constant showering of debris hitting my back. I said a brief prayer to God, and certainly only God could have heard. I knew without a doubt I was about to die. With the last words of my prayer, I passed out.

About a half-hour after the bombing had ceased, I came to. I was half-covered with leaves and other debris, and a large tree branch lay across one of my legs. At first, I was disoriented and confused. I didn't know where I was or even who I was. I only knew sudden terror. I opened my mouth to scream, but no sound came out. There was only that eerie silence that always came after the bombings, and in this instance it actually helped me to remember who and where I was.

With some effort, I slowly rolled on my back, sat up, and shoved the branch off my legs. I sat there a moment, wanting simply to be somewhere other than there. But as I regained my senses, abject fear once again washed over me.

They might be back, I thought.

In another instant, I was on my feet and running toward the shelter. In another few minutes, the door flew open and I saw the sudden fear in Father's eyes.

"You look as white as a ghost, Laura. Are you all right?"

With some coaxing, I told my brief but harrowing story. Father just shook his head, saying nothing but feeling grateful I was alive. Mother eyed me wearily, with a look I had only seen in the sick and hungry people of the streets.

"Laura, why don't you listen?"

But I refused to listen. In my very private ways, I refused to give in to the madness that now engulfed us all. These small acts of defiance were simply my way of remembering from where I had come and my way of knowing the basis for my future.

By the time we had been in Izguro a month, Mother's vacant stare had transformed itself into extreme weakness and high fever. One morning she was simply bedridden, and neither Father nor anyone else in the family knew exactly what to do for her. We tried a variety of remedies to make her more comfortable and bring down the fever, but nothing seemed to work. The wife of the Turkish man who had rented us the cottage even brought some special tea. But when, after another few days, there was still no improvement, I was sent to Candilli to get Grandmama.

Grandmama confirmed what we had all suspected. Mother was sick—very sick—and needed a doctor right away. I will never know exactly what Grandmama expected of me. Perhaps she didn't understand our situation clearly, or perhaps the urgency of her daughter's condition prompted her to seek any source of help. Regardless, that source of help was me. Father was at work, and I'm sure Grandmama felt that there was no time to waste. I took her words as an order. I was to find a doctor for Mother, but where?

I set out from our little house in Izguro with a strange combination of fear and determination. There were certainly no doctors in this little village; nor were there any in Candilli. I took what I thought was my only course. I set out for the Italian troop encampment.

The Italian soldiers were often much kinder to us than their German counterparts, and my desperation must have shown. A soldier who had sometimes helped me carry water from the well to the house in Izguro asked me what was wrong before I even spoke.

"My mother is very sick, and I need to find a doctor for her right away."

He looked at me sadly. "There are no doctors here, Laura. The nearest is in our camp at the other side of the village. Go there and ask for the Italian officer. He might be able to help you."

I ran to the other camp faster than I had ever run in my life. Still, it seemed as if the world simply stood still beneath my feet. Despite my efforts, it seemed that when the gate to the camp finally came into view, it took forever for me to reach it. My panic had turned everything into a slow-motion play of desperation.

How strange things become during times of crisis. Normally, I would have been afraid to even speak to an officer like the post commander that day. The guns and trucks and men in uniform everywhere were both intimidating and frightening to me. But desperation drives us to overcome our fears. Crisis and the flush of adrenaline has a way of eliminating reservation and strengthening the focus of resolution. Hot, sweaty, and covered with the dust of my run, I found the commander almost immediately and spoke of my plight with little hesitation. I told him that the soldier in the other camp had told me to find him, that my mother was very ill, and that I needed a doctor to see her right away.

He was a tall, rugged looking man in his fifties. But there was a warmth about him that belied his military vocation. He looked down at me with a strange combination of sadness and compassion.

"Yes, there is a doctor here, but I cannot get him to help you, little one. He is a German."

I did not understand why that should matter to me. I did not understand that the Germans hated us without knowing us. I did not understand why the man in front of me, so warm and kind, had refused my request. I began crying miserably. I told him again that my mother was very sick and needed help. I told him again about my talk with the first soldier and my long run to this place. I was sure he could see my desperation about to explode into madness.

He looked down at me still, that strange smile seeming to counteract what he had said. It was as if he was trying to tell me something without speaking. It was as if he was trying to make an innocent child understand the stupid bigotry of an adult world gone mad.

But my persistence and panic must have affected him. He pursed his lips, as if in some deep consideration of consequence. "Just a moment. Wait here."

He arrived a few minutes later with the German doctor. I again explained my situation to him, but when the Italian officer told him about my mother, he immediately said that he was not permitted to treat a Jew.

I began crying again, and between sobs I continued pleading. "No, no, please. My mother is so very sick. Please. We need your help."

I don't know whether it was my persistent crying or that the doctor felt some sort of compassion for this filthy, sweaty waif that stood before him. But he spoke again to the Italian officer, as if the two of them were conjuring a secret. I didn't hear what they said, but the doctor agreed to come to see my mother, "Just one time."

We walked back to Izguro together. I don't remember if we talked or just walked along in silence. I do remember I wasn't afraid anymore. My relief at finding a doctor far outweighed any fear of his uniform or his beliefs. Besides, I really had no idea that there was anything to be afraid of.

His visit was brief and hurried. He took some blood from my

mother, gave her some medication for her fever, and left. His entire demeanor was as if he was doing some secretive, forbidden task, and he was as far as the German authorities were concerned. There is little doubt in my mind that that doctor risked severe punishment, perhaps even death, for treating a woman who happened to be a Jew.

I will always wonder what his motivation was or if it was his at all. Was it his years of training and feelings for the sick that overcame his orders? Was it my insistent crying or perhaps the urgings of the kind Italian commander? Or was it perhaps some sort of agreement between the two of them that such an act would generate "good will" between the army and the local population? Though I think the Italian probably told the doctor he would not report his visit to the German command, I will never know for sure. I prefer to think that the doctor's compassion as a human being overcame the ridiculous dictates of his German commanders. I prefer to be forever grateful to one of the few Germans who ever showed me compassion during the war.

Three days later I returned to the encampment, and the Italian commander told me that my mother had pernicious anemia. She needed better food and lots of quiet rest. I never saw the German doctor again.

Rhodes had become such a dichotomy of lifestyles. On the one hand, we lived in constant fear. On the other, life for other nationalities went on with only small inconveniences.

Since moving to Izguro, I had become friends with a Turkish girl and her mother who were visiting the girl's grandmother on what had become an extended holiday. Because the girl's father was an officer in the Turkish army and because they were protected through the Turkish embassy, they were "fortunate enough" to be observers of our plight, but not participants. I wish I remembered their names, for they were kind and generous to me.

I remember conversations with the girl in the village, and I often helped her tend to the few animals her grandmother owned. Since I needed to stay out of the house so Mother could have quiet while she recuperated, the girl and I spent long hours talking and enjoying each other's company.

If only we had been in the village under different circumstances. Except for the ever-present soldiers and occasional airborne reminders of war, life here was simple and serene. Even food was more plentiful than in the city, for we at least had milk products and eggs that were produced locally. And some of the soldiers sold us canned meat and chocolate from the black market. While we were not permitted to buy from the market ourselves, the Italians would often get such items for us secretly, for many of them were compassionate and kind people. For their generosity, I will be forever grateful.

The Turkish girl's mother was tall and graceful and had obviously come from an educated and well-to-do family. Even in my darkest personal moments, she would always greet me with a smile and was always willing to sit and listen to my problems. She was almost like a temporary mother to me while mine was sick. In the world that Rhodes had become, where children like us were easily forgotten and overlooked, she always paid attention. While time and what I have endured prevent me somehow from recalling their names, I will always remember the Turkish girl and her mother and the smile in their eyes.

Seven German SS troops came to Rhodes in July 1944. Within a few days, Father and Joseph came home and told us that all the Jewish men between the ages of 14 and 50 had been ordered to report to the Italian Air Force headquarters the next morning. They didn't know why they had to do this, but they told us not to fear.

As dusk settled on Izguro that next day, I found myself sitting alone in front of our house. The air hung heavy and still, and it seemed there wasn't a single sound, save the crickets awakening to forage. The sun was now just a faint glow shrouded by the dark, and Father and Joseph still had not returned. It seemed that as my fear grew, the world around me had become ripe and ominous, like that hot, late summer moment before the apple falls from the tree. I fidgeted anxiously, staring down the path that led to the house in hopes that Father would appear.

But it was not to be. The next day German soldiers came through the villages and ordered us to the headquarters as well. We were told to bring our valuables and jewelry, too, because we would need them to help us relocate at our new destination.

Mother was far too weak to walk only a few yards, let alone the long distance to the Air Force headquarters. I helped her to the bus that ran between the villages and Rhodes.

A few hours later I returned to the village by myself to gather the few valuables we still had. As I left the bus and walked down the little road between the houses of Izguro, the Turkish woman and her daughter stood waiting for me.

"Laura, we want you to stay with us. We will hide you as a part of our family. We will keep you safe here."

"My family needs me. I have to report."

The Turkish woman shook her head with a look of worry. She seemed to know my fate, though I had no idea.

"Please, Laura, stay with us. We will take you to Turkey. Your father has family there, yes? Please, Laura. You will be safe with us."

I hugged her and could feel her tremble as she began to weep. I could sense her fear for me, but I was ignorant of my own. I would be with my family, and as long as I was, I would be safe.

"I can't," I whispered. "They need me."

I returned to our house, gathered a small purse of jewelry, and began walking toward the headquarters. As we walked, the girl and her mother continued to plead for me to stay. I had no idea of my plight, only that I needed to be with Father and Mother.

As we walked along, a young German soldier passed by. The things one remembers in times of stress are so strange. He was blond and very handsome, but it was his look that I will always recall. He looked sadly puzzled and deeply moved by the weight of some decision. He wasn't intimidating or frightening, and I know from his demeanor that he harbored no hate. But that look was sad and pointless. It was a look of war, I think. A look of futility; of longing for the peace of home and family, of the hopelessness of having to do things one didn't believe in, regardless of which side one was on. I suppose there were many looks like that in those years. I suppose I had that look now and again. But I will always remember his. He might have been eating better than I, but his mind was invaded by the same demons as mine had. The source of his fears might have been different from mine, but they were borne of the same insane devil of war.

By the time we reached the headquarters, the Turkish woman had become nearly hysterical. She cried loudly, holding me tightly, begging me to stay. She pulled at me, and I struggled with her.

"I could not live without knowing what is to become of my family."

"Stay," she begged. "Stay with us Laura!"

"I cannot! I must not."

With a strong pull, I broke free of her, turned quickly, and walked into the building. I looked back as I reached the top of the steps and the door, and the woman and her daughter were walking away slowly, still obviously crying. Clearly, they knew, or at least had an idea, of my fate. But I knew nothing, save fear for my mother's health and fear of the unknown. There were no rumors for teenage girls to know. There was no way I could understand the horrors I would see. I knew nothing, but the woman and girl whose names I forget will remain in my heart as long as it stirs.

As I walked in the doors, I was struck by the hot, humid air in the building. I doubt anyone noticed my entry, for there seemed to be hundreds of people in a very large room. They stood to my left in groups along the length of the room, talking and arguing chaotically. But my attention was riveted to my right. Within a few feet of me stood two men. The first was short, very fat, and bald. In a uniform that seemed too small for his pig-like countenance, he seemed to leer at every person in the room, all at once. He was like a hungry swine, straining at its harness at the sight of garbage about to be devoured. And the people of the Juderia were but pieces of rot to him. Just so much worthless feed for a worthless cause.

The second man stood tall and lean. A man, whom I came to later believe was Kurt Wolhaim, was in full dress uniform, what looked like SS pins gleaming on his lapels, his tall boots shined to perfection. He seemed at parade rest, legs somewhat apart and hands clasped behind his back. He smiled contentedly, as if all was right with the world. With his crisp confidence, he seemed to be keeping the mad pig at bay with an invisible harness. They spoke in muted tones, the pig and the officer, surveying with their disparate forms of pleasure the plunder of humanity before them.

And plunder there was. In front of them were large sacks of money and four wooden barrels filled with jewelry. And I, like they, stood transfixed at the sight of it. Someone took my purse from me, and I'm sure its contents found their way into the barrels. But I remember little of it, for the hoard before me seemed greater than any pirate's treasure I had imagined. We could only have stood there for seconds, the pig, the officer, the plunder, and I, but the eerie sight of it all became etched in my memory as if in some slow-motion picture. It has been more than fifty years since those seconds passed, but the movie still plays sometimes in my nightmares.

For some reason, the gypsy woman's fortune came to my mind. I remembered her frightening words about strange uniforms and danger. I could feel my insides twist and turn in sudden fear. In an instant, I moved into the crowd, for the first time sensing that attention from these odd twins of hatred was something to avoid.

At first I couldn't find anyone in the family. There were so many people, and it was somewhat difficult to move about without catching the notice of the pig or the officer, or at least imagining you would. But I found Auntie Diana in the restroom. She was flushing a special bracelet, her *mania de chaton*, down the toilet. I gasped at first, but she just turned to me and smiled wryly.

"Somehow I doubt they're taking our valuables for safekeeping." Auntie turned briefly, tossing a small ring into the toilet. "I'll not have these Germans using *my* jewelry for their fun."

Everything else that afternoon in the headquarters was blurred. I don't remember how Auntie Diana and I found the rest of the family, what we were told to do, or how we were treated. I only remember being scared and thinking constantly of the gypsy's words.

The people stretched out from the headquarters building as far as I could see. Two thousand of us walked through Rhodes to the port, carrying belongings or little children, in a long, shuffling line. It was hot that day, and it seemed the sun pierced every corner and avenue, even those shaded, narrow streets between the buildings of home. Before too long, people began leaving things along the road. How odd this all was. Like a mile-long herd of sheep, we trudged along in the heat, irrevocably locked together by an invisible chain of our own loyalty and ignorance. These were the same streets we had danced on. These were the same whitewashed houses we had laughed in together. This was the same sun that had shone brightly on our simple, rustic lives.

But the sun had turned savage, and the dust we stirred up as we walked turned our view of the city dirty. In a single afternoon, home had become a foreign place. Here and there, people gathered in small groups to watch us. They were Greeks, mostly, and a few of them shouted at us as we passed.

"It's good they are taking you from Rhodes. Go away. Do not come back."

The same bomb that had torn away Cousin Moise's leg had severely damaged our synagogue, and the crater in La Kay Ancha was but one of many that pockmarked the Juderia. But though we didn't know it, our passing that day marked its complete obliteration. More surely than a thousand bombs or the worst of earthquakes, our slow walk through its streets emptied it of its last vestiges of life. Home had become a damaged, empty shell, and I wondered if Great-grandmama Strea wept for us from her lonely place on the wall. It was the oddest of good-byes, for most of us thought we would return. We were packed aboard three small ships and, by that evening, we departed Rhodes forever.

3.

TERROR

AS DUSK APPROACHED, Rhodes slowly faded into the Aegean. Scared
and cold, I still noticed the strange quiet that had overcome the ship.
Earlier in the day there had been many anxious voices and complaints of discomfort; now there was only the occasional whimper of
a child and the constant low drumming of the ship's propeller.

I had no sense of when my friend Laurina appeared or how long
I'd been watching Rhodes's slow dip into the sea. But somehow, I
knew that everyone else was watching, too. They were so very quiet,
like the glassy spread of the Aegean around them. And as dusk slowly
gave way to the darkness, it was for me as if the last glimmer of color
in my life was slowly fading away. I wondered if I would awaken
tomorrow to a black-and-white world, like the movies we used to
watch in the theater.

There had always been a deeply superstitious side to the Jewish
people of Rhodes. Many took very seriously the results of palm read-
ings and tarot card sessions with the gypsies. And there were a thousand quotes and actions based on the folklore of both Jewish kabala
and the rich traditions of our Greek and Turkish neighbors.

But this foreboding was far different from the bad news of a palm
reader. I struggled to contain my foreboding from becoming outright
terror, for as I looked in the eyes of the adults around me, I saw only
the reflections of my own uncertainty.

Yet the ships didn't frighten me, nor did the rumors of submarines
that sank them these days. It was that uncertainty of tomorrow and
the places I'd never seen. It was the tension I sensed in my parents
and friends and the rumors of what the Germans did to Jews. It was

the chill in the air and the shivering I couldn't control. Most of all, it was Rhodes, fading now from the colors of life to the blackness of night. Our island, so full of life, was now but an empty shell sinking into the sea.

A very old woman nearby began to wail, as if she was mourning at a funeral. And as dusk slowly faded to a starlit sky, her crying became more and more hysterical. Grandmama tried to comfort her, but it was as if she had lost all sense of who she was. It was as if, ripped away from the only home she had known, insanity now poured in to fill the void in her consciousness.

It became too dark to see Rhodes anymore. I looked at Laurina and saw her eyes were filled with tears. By now, I was too cold to notice my own.

During daylight hours, the three ships anchored in the lee of islands and along shorelines to avoid detection by aircraft and, particularly, the ever-present submarines patrolling the Mediterranean. Torpedoes were a constant fear of the ships' crews, and they did not hesitate to make those fears known to us. "These ships you are on are nothing more than tramp steamers," the soldiers would say, "but we are slow and vulnerable. Just one torpedo and we are in big trouble. You must all remember this even when we travel at night. The sounds we make can all be heard underneath the sea."

Our normal waking hours were spent in increasing filth and fear. Nearly seven hundred people were crowded into a ship designed to carry cargo and a crew of six and, with a stop at the island of Kos to pick up another hundred of us, we became even more crowded. For the most part, families stayed together in small groups huddled on the deck or in the hold. Men lucky enough to be on deck simply urinated over the side. Inevitably, small piles of feces began to appear in every corner of the ship, and the smell of hundreds of people without the opportunity to bathe or change their clothes would have been overwhelming had we all not been immersed in it.

As time passed, tempers became raw. There was much arguing and occasional fighting over what in ordinary circumstances would have been totally unimportant. Families that were close on Rhodes became bitter and quietly argued over space on the deck. Women sometimes became angry enough to claw at each other over otherwise ridiculous issues. By the time we neared our destination, the smallest look or gesture quickly became a source of loud irritation and argument.

What little food that was available was rationed carefully. Typically, my one meal each day consisted of boiled turnip broth, which I hated, and occasionally a piece of hard bread. There was often mold on the bread that had to be broken off, and the broth soon fomented bouts of diarrhea among many of us.

Aside from the ever-present fear of submarines, I much preferred the night. At least we were moving toward a destination. At least the stagnant, hot air of the day gave way to a cool, sometimes cold breeze as we sailed through the darkness.

Our family had been fortunate to be huddled on deck instead of in the hot misery of the hold. Father and Mother, Grandmama, and the rest of us stood and sat in an eight-foot-square area at the stern of the ship. Despite the constant thumping we suffered from the turns of the propeller at night and our exposure to the elements, we were far more comfortable, particularly during the hot afternoon, than those below. There, several of the elderly died of the heat or a combination of it and any of several other maladies related to their plight. The rabbis' complaints to the contrary, bodies were unceremoniously dumped overboard each evening as soon as the ships were underway. That practice had begun with the old woman who cried as we watched Rhodes fade into the sea. Within an hour of darkness she died and was the first of many to be thrown over the side by the ship's crew. They had no other choice. There was little room for the living, let alone the dead.

It was only 250 miles from Rhodes to our destination of Piraeus, but with constant fear of submarines and a stop at the island of Kos to pick up Jews there, the trip took eight days. For me, it was a time of feeling as if my very soul had been stripped from me. Like the rest of what remained of the Juderia, I had become nothing more than a speck on the vast Aegean Sea. Pulled relentlessly by the forces of war and hate over which we had no control, I had become part of what would be a forgotten statistic. Just another small bit of culture torn apart and awash in the seas of war.

I stared up at a starless sky. For the moment, I was reassured by Asher's steady breathing and the constant deep rumble of the propeller. My mind wandered back to Father's stories. And as the sounds of the sea against the sides of the ship came to me, as the cold breeze again washed over me, I thought of Nino. Numbly, I wondered where he had gone, whether he missed me as much as I longed after him, and what those blue eyes were seeing. I hoped that Nino was in a better place than I. He had to be. He just had to be. In my last moments of consciousness before sleep, Nino's blue eyes faded off into the darkness. I curled myself around Asher as our three little ships plowed on into the black Aegean night.

Stella woke me. "Look, Laura, can you see? It's a boat."

The ships had pulled in to the island of Leros during the waning hours of darkness. Uncharacteristically, most of us had slept through the usual commotion associated with stopping and dropping anchor. Now, in the very first light of dawn, a small boat approached. There were two men aboard, one sitting in the stern and one standing amidship. I could see that the man standing was tall and dark, dressed in a white shirt and dark pants. I mused that he looked as if he were about to go to a formal dinner. The boat came alongside just forward of where our family was huddled.

They motored very slowly alongside the ship. The man standing began passing a few loaves of bread and sticks of hard salami to the grateful passengers. Strangely, there was no arguing or fighting over these foodstuffs, limited as they were. I remember that Father had caught one loaf of bread, tossed by the man in the white shirt. He had quickly broken it in half and passed it to a group standing next to us. Within moments, it seemed as if somehow those few loaves of bread and salamis had found their way to the mouths of everyone on the ship. I thought numbly about the story of God's gift of manna in the desert. Even stranger, the crew said nothing at the obvious gesture of humanity by the men in the boat and took no food for themselves. Perhaps they knew it would be one of the last acts of kindness any of us would ever see. Perhaps they knew how far a few pieces of bread would go in keeping us calm and under control. It didn't matter. Eagerly, I stuffed a small piece of bread in my mouth. It wasn't a lot different from what we'd received along with the daily turnip broth. But it was, at least, fresh and soft. It tasted better than anything I could remember. The kindness of the two men on the boat, whatever their motivation, made the bread sweet.

I was later to find out that the captain of our crowded ship had been responsible for the appearance of the boat alongside. When we stopped in Kos, he had angrily argued with the authorities that he would go no farther than Leros unless better food was provided for those on board. It was testimony, I guess, to both the kindness of rational people who could see our plight and the anxiousness of the

Germans to do away with us. How ironic they would give us sustenance only to murder so many of us a few weeks later.

But that numb foreboding washed over me again. I was close enough to the side of the ship to see clearly the boat and the men in it. They both smiled at the people on the ship, exchanging short words of greeting with our gratitude. They even laughed on occasion. But I could see their eyes. I could see a sadness there like I had never seen in anyone. It was a look of unbelievable hopelessness and pity. Even though I was too hungry, cold, and emotionally numb to care, the look in those eyes pierced my consciousness. Long after the boat had left us, long after the sun had risen and made us all begin to sweat, I sat huddled on the deck, shivering in fear.

In time, I regained control. Somehow, the all-encompassing fear that washed over me was slowly displaced, and by late afternoon, I finally stopped shaking. But it had been a long internal battle that had sapped much of my strength. There had been moments that day when I simply knew I would die, even wanted to die to escape the fear. But in the end, the foundation of my will, built of the simple beliefs and hopes of upbringing, had proven too strong for my fear to tear down. In the end, I had remembered from where I had come, and from deep within that rustic simplicity, I found a small glimmer of hope. It sustained me, like the piece of bread I had hours earlier. It brought me back from the brink of an abyss I now too clearly understood, an abyss created by unbelievable hate and fueled by the unknown.

I felt tired as never before. I looked numbly at our family but found strength in their presence. At least they were here, suffering this misery with me. At least I could take comfort in that. As hollow as they all looked, I realized that my foundation had not been built in Rhodes, but in the hearts of the people around me. We were all in this together. We all huddled here together. Whatever misery tomorrow might force on us, we would share it. We would learn from it. We would build new foundations for new Lauras based on it.

As tired as I was, I found the strength to care about the people I loved. Father had said so little since we'd boarded the ship. It was as if he had lost his soul, and his will with it. His movements and actions seemed to be based more on instinct and practice than on conscious thought. Much of the time he simply stood staring off the stern of ship, as if that last view of Rhodes still filled his mind. I could not fully understand his despair, but I felt it. I knew that inside, he stood on the edge of that same abyss I'd stared into.

The voyage had been hard on Mother. Her condition had obviously worsened, and she coughed continually. At night, someone in the family always managed to share a coat with her to keep her warm, but it hadn't seemed to help. She was gaunt, and her blackened eyes made her appear frighteningly close to death. It was difficult to look in her eyes, for I saw nothing there. Beyond hope, beyond hopelessness, there was only a resigned acceptance of fate. I knew that the person who had been such a source of strength and learning for all of us was now only a shell. I wanted to hold her, to touch her, to be able to infuse strength and hope again in those hopeless eyes. But it was too late for that. Long before we had left Rhodes, I had thought long and hard about Mother's sickness and had found a way to accept Mother's death, should it occur. It meant pulling away. It meant holding my mother at arm's length, as much as I wanted to wrap my arms around her. It was even more important now. As selfish as it made me feel, I knew Mother understood. I had simply begun to say good-bye, and Mother gave me the strength to do it. I touched her hand and managed to smile. But I couldn't look in Mother's eyes.

With Father's withdrawn countenance, Grandmama had been the main source of strength and maturity for us. She found a way to provide encouragement, such as encouragement was, for everyone. She doted on Mother constantly. I thought that perhaps she found strength in everyone else's weakness, that perhaps she now knew why she had survived all these years. More than at any time, Grandmama was there when it mattered the most. At one time or another during this voyage, we all found an escape, however brief, in Grandmama's arms.

My brothers and sister seemed fearful and remote. Perhaps they waged the same inner battles I did. I hoped they found strength from whatever inner source they had, and I quietly vowed to give what hope I could. Whatever the outcome of our combined futures, I knew we would survive if we could be together. The results of our separation might be far less certain.

For the first time ever, I had seen fear in Uncle Rahamin's eyes. But I had also seen anger, and from that anger I knew he would be all right. It was Uncle Rahamin who whispered questions as to why we didn't rise up and take control of the ship. It was Uncle Rahamin who appeared ready to give everything, including life itself if necessary, in that quest. It was Uncle Rahamin who fearfully accepted Uncle Shumuel's answers to his question.

"Where would we go, back to Rhodes and the Nazis there, if we could find our way, Rahamin? What would we do for our wives and children when the Germans came looking for the ship? Most of us are old, young, or weak. How could we fight a sustained battle to survive, and with what? An old ship and our fists? We have no choice, Rahamin. We have no choice in this but to hope things are better where we are going. The risks to our families otherwise are just too great."

With that discussion, Uncle Rahamin had become resigned to accept the fate of the many. From my perspective, though, it was as if a tree had been stripped of its leaves. I remembered how much passion for life Uncle Rahamin had always seemed to have. I remembered his exuberant wisdom, like that day with Jaco under the Amora tree. I remembered with sadness, for both appeared to have been taken from him. He harbored now only a resigned anger, a resentment of the captors he couldn't control, and the people he couldn't convince to fight.

The rest of the family—Auntie Diana, Auntie Fortune with baby Mattie, and little Jaco—seemed to withdraw progressively from normal interactions. It was as if something was dying in each of them, gradually drawing them away with it. Whether it was the strain of the voyage, the fear, or the longing for Rhodes I could only guess. But still, we remained together. Somehow I realized that it was all that remained for any of us.

I curled myself on the deck. Together, I thought, we can endure this. Together we must. Tomorrow will rely on our togetherness and what we bring to it from Rhodes. In moments, I was asleep.

At some time during our voyage, it was the same for every family stuffed aboard those three little ships. Other Lauras found strength and hope. Other fathers withdrew in guilt and indecision. Other grandmamas found meaning and infused life in those around them. Their foundations in Rhodes were alternately a source of strength and of weakness. The simplicity of life and the closeness of the Juderia gave many of them a fundamental base on which to persevere together. The sheltered nature of our existence made most of us totally unprepared for the realities we would face. Those days aboard the ships were the transition, for each of us, from one life to the other.

I awoke to a hot, dry wind. I sat up with a start, for it was daylight and the ship was still running. "We're coming in to Piraeus." It was Uncle Rahamin, pointing toward the starboard side of the ship. "I can see the buildings."

Father stared off into the distance. "We could have been in Palestine instead of here."

Slowly, the ships came into port, mooring behind one another at a long wooden pier that ran along the shoreline. I could see the men in uniforms waiting for us. They seemed to glare up at me, to leer, salivating in anticipation. I shuddered, ignoring their stares in recognition that they were staring at everyone, not just me. I reminded myself not to be afraid. I thought of home for a moment, but the innocence of Rhodes paled against the glint of the SS officers' guns. By now, though, I was accustomed to this battle with myself. I knew I could control my fear, that I must, in order to endure. I took a deep breath and, with the family, haltingly walked down the gangplank.

The pier was filled with people and soldiers barking orders. Dogs strained at leashes, but seemed less vicious than their masters. That hot, dry wind blew clouds of dust and debris the length of the pier, and there seemed to be paper blowing everywhere. There was no color to this, I thought, just differing shades of gray and grit. It was surreal, but frighteningly real.

We became a mass of shuffling humanity, herded down the pier by angry shepherds without care for their flock. There were few protests and no shouts of defiance, just the stooped movement of men and women and confused children, accompanied by the quick shock of occasional gunshots and the bark of the dogs. There was, perhaps, a semblance of logic in our cowering acceptance of the Nazis' brutality. Beyond self-preservation, the realm of the flock was one of the last bits of civility amid this inferno of confusion.

But the young were not the only confused children among us. The elderly were just as frightened and uncertain as the little ones, and they refused to leave the docks when told to do so. I began to understand the callousness of our captors. I began to understand their utter disdain for our culture and our lives. I didn't see them die. I only heard the shots as their small group was lined up and executed where they stood.

Still together, we found ourselves huddled with hundreds of others in a broad, open courtyard. This was Haidary, one of those small, Nazi-controlled concentration camps scattered like a pox across Europe from the Mediterranean to the North Sea. They found Haidary and other camps like it a convenient place for murder, torture, rape, and, as the title implied, the concentration of Jews and other prisoners for eventual shipment to more efficient places of death. But Haidary was our introduction to the Nazis' bestiality, and it had a death-rattle message all its own. Before I was formally introduced to its butchery, I heard many screams and cries from behind those courtyard walls. We were not the only ones here. We were not the only people huddling in fear.

Uncle Rahamin had wandered through our sitting mass trying to find either food or water. I could taste the dry mixture of dust and salt caking my lips. I found myself looking down at nothing, but noticed that everyone else had a similar countenance. Looks were exchanged from this cowering position, for the people already feared the attention of their shepherds. And in this way I sat for hours, feeling only fear and thinking of little else.

There was an open wall at the east side of the courtyard where the Nazis had not permitted anyone to sit. They seemed to congregate near that wall, watching their captives casually, barking orders and barking dogs combining in a knife-like cacophony. If anyone had doubted the need to remain unobtrusive, these Nazis casually made it clear that they had less than no regard for us. There was no explanation, no sadness, no emotion. There was only the bark of the dogs, the strange sounding words of the guards and officers, and the punctuation of gunshots. Beginning with the rabbis, anyone the Germans knew or thought held a position of leadership was systematically brought to the wall, tied, and shot. I shuddered each time I heard them but continued to stare at the ground. My mind ran away from the horror of watching people die. My thoughts were numbed by the lack of food and water. But an occasional sideways glance at the wall reminded me of our new-found place. What had been people I knew and friends I loved now mingled on the wall, shreds of tissue mixed in a deep red stain of blood.

Uncle Rahamin had not been successful in finding food, but he did return with a small container of water. He carefully rationed it to the family, and each of us took just a small sip from the rusty cup. The water tasted warm and brackish, but I welcomed it, for the liquid at least washed away the grit and dust from my splitting lips. Over the next 48 hours, an occasional sip of water would be the only sustenance for me or any of the others huddling in the courtyard.

Nazi guards regularly wandered through the crowd, constantly watchful for the slightest excuse to extinguish yet another life against the wall. And unlike the rest of the immediate family, Uncle Rahamin defied his captors, if only to the extent that he didn't cower as much as the others. During our time in the courtyard, he regularly searched for water or bits of food, and he was unafraid to stop and help others huddled along his way in any way that he could. But his new-found hate for the Germans was too apparent. He whispered continuous complaints about their condition, frequently accompanied by outlandish schemes for their escape. He glared at our captors, turning his stare away just before it was returned.

It was, perhaps, the only time in those two days that I looked up for more than a moment. It was, certainly, the only few minutes where my numb, thoughtless state was broken. Frustrated at being unable to find food, Uncle Rahamin was complaining bitterly, his whispered epithets against the Nazis sputtered through clenched teeth. "They will kill us all unless we do something now! We are weak, but many. If we would all just rise up, we could overpower these bastards."

I heard and saw the guard out of the corner of my eye. There was a quick, gritty scraping sound as his boots spun about from behind Uncle Rahamin. Though I didn't move, my eyes looked up and to my left where he stood, just a dozen feet away from us. In an instant, he covered the space, shouting, "You!" as he approached.

Just as Uncle Rahamin turned his head, he caught the force of the guard's rifle butt against his back. I sat staring, transfixed. I didn't know whether my words were spoken or thought, but it didn't matter. "This can't be happening! This can't be happening!" Over and over came the words, racing from my mind at a pace as fast as my panicky heartbeat. The impact of the blow buckled Uncle Rahamin to the ground, and he groaned in pain. The guard, now standing over him, glowered menacingly.

There are moments when fear and abject horror combine to make time slow to a point where it nearly stops. Though the guard's strike at Uncle Rahamin occurred in little more than a few seconds, everything I saw seemed to be happening with agonizingly slow motion. The adrenaline coursing through me made me gasp, and each heartbeat felt as if a sledgehammer was slowly pounding against my chest, rocking me violently. The guard's words seemed slurred, coming in a deep, low voice that seemed as much to be emanating from some unbelievably evil ghost.

"Get up. Get up!" he shouted, the words spilling from a face that had a look of bizarre insanity. He could not have been much older than me, his thin frame and signs of acne showing his youth. Yet he was filled with the power his arrogant peers had given him that his rifle enforced. I was incredulous, for while the guard brutalized Uncle Rahamin with both weapon and words, he smiled. He was enjoying this. He was having fun.

My fear drove a stake through me, pinned me to the spot, froze me in a stare of horror. Yet through it all, a strange calm overtook me. It was a feeling I somehow knew would come many times again. It was the calm of acceptance. Though every bit of me was in a state of horrible turmoil, though every fear I had ever had was now combined and magnified tenfold by what we watched, I let my fear wash over me. I suddenly found myself accepting it and, in so doing, was able to detach from the moment, was able to protect a very small piece of Laura. I suppose Uncle will soon join the rabbis, I thought. I suppose I am insane.

The guard shouted again at Uncle Rahamin, as others nearby scuffled away from the scene as best they could. "Get up!"

But Uncle Rahamin could barely move. I thought for a moment that the guard would simply shoot him where he lay. But in that slow-motion few seconds, it became obvious that his frustration with Uncle overtook his detached ability simply to kill and mutilate. Quickly slinging the rifle over his shoulder, he roughly grabbed at Uncle by the collar, using both hands, and began pulling him to his feet.

Everything at that moment became confused and chaotic. From another few feet away, there were shouts and horrible screams. A tall, heavy man, being taken by an officer to what he obviously knew was the wall, suddenly turned and grabbed at the officer's pistol. In the struggle, the gun went off, and the bullet ripped through the arm of a woman and shattered the skull of her young son.

Amid the blood-spattered screams surrounding the little boy's faceless, convulsing body, the struggle between the man and the officer continued. The pistol, held tightly by both of them, fired several more times, bullets finding random targets in the crowd or in the courtyard walls. Dropping Uncle Rahamin in a heap, the guard quickly ran over to assist his officer, ending the struggle with his rifle butt to the back of the man's head.

Together, the officer and the guard dragged the unconscious man toward the wall, where he was shot as soon as he regained consciousness. Within a few minutes, several guards returned to retrieve the body of the little boy and another woman who had been killed in the melee. But those only wounded, like the young boy's mother, were simply left to cope with their new infirmities with whatever means they had. Though the pain of his wounds would not leave him for several days, Uncle Rahamin was one of those ignored.

There would be many times in the coming months when Uncle Rahamin would wish his life had simply ended in a few spatters against the courtyard wall. From light to dark in an instant. No pain. No anguish at seeing others brutalized and murdered. No nightmare memories of what would follow. But those thoughts were yet to be created. For now, an overwhelming combination of relief and despair overtook him. Selfishly thankful at being spared, his relief became confused with the uncontrollable guilt he felt. Though his intellect told him that utter chance had spared his life, something inside told him there was more to it than that. Something inside flushed him with remorse and guilt for the man who struggled, whose life now dribbled in red rivulets down the courtyard wall, instead of his.

Had they cared to keep him alive, the Nazis could not possibly have conceived a better strategy to subdue Uncle Rahamin's rebelliousness. The utter brutality of those few moments made him realize the dire consequence of action, any action of any kind. For while this small, brutal scene in a play called the Holocaust was choreographed by chance, Uncle Rahamin now knew that action led to opportunities for chance to occur. These days, chance manifested itself as the Grim Reaper. Uncle had looked in its face and had been ignored. But he had watched its indiscriminate murder of the innocent all around him. He now knew the rules of this deadly game of chance.

With each passing hour, the plight of the people of the Juderia became more hopeless and extreme, as in previous years the plight of countless other Jews from Europe and the Mediterranean had, moment by moment, deteriorated at the hands of the Nazis. But by a strange twist of German efficiency, the future of these deportees to the death camps was even more bleak than that of their predecessors. The death machine had become too efficient. The camps, stretched beyond capacity as a result of the effectiveness of the SS in rounding up Jews, were growing in population faster than the crematoriums could burn them. As a result, a decrease in the numbers actually reaching the camps was encouraged. The Nazi bureaucracy quietly urged those along the transfer routes subtly to work that game of chance Uncle Rahamin had recently learned. Little wonder, then, that the courtyard wall remained a busy place of massacre. Little wonder I shuddered often from the sound of gunshots. After the war Haidary would be called "The Bastille of Greece."

But I would soon learn to control my flinching. I would soon come to regard the sound of gunfire as an everyday occurrence. Like Uncle Rahamin, I would soon construe every death I saw as just another small scene in a much larger play. The only difference was whether I or my family would be part of the audience of one of the actors. The route from here to Auschwitz was fast becoming littered with the bodies of actors from every conceivable scene of insanity.

Moments seemed like hours, and hours seemed but seconds. I had lost any sense of time. I just sat quietly lost in thoughtlessness, alternately sleeping fitfully and waking to a dulled sense of reality, brought to frightening crispness by the occasional murder of my friends.

It ended without thought, without emotion, and without any sensation of what happened. I simply found myself walking, with a thousand others, through the streets of Piraeus. I wondered if I had been walking in my sleep and had just now awoken to the dust and grit of yet another journey to nowhere. My body ached, stiff from sitting for so very long.

We seemed to be shuffling through an abandoned city. There were no people on the streets, no faces peering out the windows at us. There were only the Nazi guards, brutally urging us to hurry, and often ensuring progress with their rifle butts. The white buildings reminded me of La Kay Ancha, the marketplace at home. But there was no laughter here. There were no merchants here. There was nothing here but the buildings that framed a long empty street to oblivion. I noticed I was wearing the same dress I had been wearing when we left Rhodes. I wondered dumbly if my body odor would offend anyone.

I had no idea how far we'd walked or how long it had taken to pass down that long quiet street. For the most part, I had simply walked along with the rest of the family, watching my feet move step after step, whispering occasional words as much to myself as to anyone around me.

The long line slowed, stopped, then started again haltingly as we rounded a corner into a narrow street. An antiaircraft battery, manned by a half-dozen men, was perched atop a two-story building at the corner. I stared up at it, long barrels pointing menacingly toward the sky. An officer, I thought, peered vigilantly through binoculars, watching the sky constantly for any sign of aircraft. I had heard no sirens since we'd arrived in Piraeus, nor had I felt the deep rumble of bombs, even distantly. Nonetheless, there were obvious signs that war had come to Greece. A few of the buildings we had passed were burned-out shells, and here and there we had to walk over debris that littered the street.

I remembered the bombings in Rhodes and that helplessness as the bombs fell. For a moment, I hoped the officer's eyes were keen, for as much as I hated them, I knew instinctively that somehow they would keep me alive, even if only by circumstance. For all the fear, for all the absolute horror of this, I knew that death was not my destiny—at least not now.

But what of the others? What of Grandmama, and Father, and all the rest? For the first time, standing on that corner, I realized that the awful nausea that had stayed with me since we'd left Rhodes was not borne of a sense of fear for self. My shivering had not begun because I thought I might die.

Rhodes had already been stripped away, and the last piece of my reality lay in the hearts of family and friends. One by one, the Nazis were taking those pieces away. How long would it be before someone very close to me was exterminated? I shuddered. What would life be like if I had to live it alone? I could feel myself losing control again, and I was quick to rationalize that hope was still with us. Mother and Father were still here and so was the rest of the family. I found myself praying they would somehow survive, and that vigilant officer gave me a momentary sense of security. But underlying my rational thought, that pervasive fear remained. My struggle just to survive was matched by an inner struggle to believe that life would be worth living if I did.

I stared blankly at the officer and realized that my gaze was being returned. A young Italian soldier, standing on the roof a few feet away from the emplacement, was looking directly at me. My eyes shifted to him momentarily, then away as fear of attention overtook me.

"It's all right. Don't be afraid." I heard his shout from the rooftop and knew my fearful gaze had been recognized among the fearful stare of hundreds.

"The trains will take you to work, and away from the war. Don't be afraid."

The incongruity of the young soldier's words struck me like a sledgehammer. Even those working with our captors were not permitted to see the truth! I thought of the gunshots and the blood on the wall. That anyone could believe our survival was anything more than a convenience to the Nazis was simply unimaginable. I wanted to shout back to him. Wanted to raise my fists to him and scream of the murder I had already seen.

"Then why do they shoot our rabbis?" It was a man at the edge of the line, just ahead of me, who obviously had the same rage at the soldier's words that I did. With a suddenness that surprised me, one of the guards hit him almost before he had finished the sentence. The blow of the pistol grip crumpled him, and he lay on the ground unconscious as the line began to move.

The short narrow street we had turned onto opened now to a rail yard. Long rows of boxcars greeted us, and the guards were already herding the people through the open doors. I could sense the fear in the crowd around me. Most of us had never seen a train before, and no one knew exactly where we were being taken. There were only the guards and their rifles and the ever-present dogs, joined now by the intimidating lines of rail cars. There were few words. There was no confusion and noise as there had been at the docks. Instead, there was only the eerie sound of a thousand shuffling souls and the grating noise of the rail car doors being shut against the future of most of them.

Even before the guards slammed the door, the interior of the box-car was humid, musty, and insufferably hot. The old and young were crammed into every inch of space. The car smelled of cattle, with dry straw covering most of the floor. Two buckets stood toward the rear of the car. One was empty, and the other filled with water. There was nothing else.

It was as if every person in that boxcar had withdrawn into some inner place, lost in this sea of war and inhumanity, unwilling to speak a single word of the turmoil within. No words were spoken as the door slammed closed. There were only the sounds of the coughing of the sick and the whimper of a child sitting on the floor near the buckets. A dull light shone on a few of the people, cast mainly from the small ventilation ports along the upper walls of the car.

I held Stella's hand in a slimy clasp of dust and sweat. Father, Mother, Grandmama and Asher sat quietly nearby. I mused that Uncle Rahamin and Auntie Diana, holding little Mattie and Jaco close by her, were still wearing the same clothes we had left Rhodes in. I suppose I was too numb to notice that neither I nor anyone else had had a chance to change clothing, much less bathe. Almost as soon as the door had been closed, the temperature in the car began to rise, and the smell of livestock was quickly replaced by the stifling odors of suffering people. I glanced at an old man, illuminated by the light from the port above where I stood. Even in the semidarkness, I could see the sweat trickling down his forehead. I blinked thoughtlessly as the salt from my own perspiration dribbled into my eyes. And there I remained, staring blankly, for the rest of the afternoon. By the time the train was loaded, the door had been closed nearly five hours. I felt at times as if there was not enough air in the car to breathe, as if we would all suffocate at any moment. But this was not my time, and I knew it. This was only another part in the play. I suffered through the act quietly, drenched in my own sweat, covered with the grime of our journey, and immersed in the abyss of hopelessness. The only thing I heard anyone in the family say came from Father.

"We could have been in Palestine by now."

"Laura!"

Was someone calling my name?

"Laura! Laura!" I turned around to peer through the small barred window. Although my view was limited, I could see that there were still many people on the loading dock.

"Laura!"

And there he was, pushing here and there to attempt to see inside the cars.

"Nino!"

He turned and saw my face barely visible through the window. He was close enough that I could see that look in his eyes and the tears streaming down his cheeks. Through the quiet, shuffling confusion that marked the activities outside, he stood out like a tall rocky spire in an unsettled sea. He just stood there, motionless in that quiet sea of sadness. We didn't say anything, for we didn't need to. He obviously knew our destination, and I instantly knew the depth of his love in those few moments of tears. How strange life is sometimes. How odd the instance of coincidence or destiny. Though I will never know for sure, I suspect that Nino knew beforehand that the Jews from Rhodes were being deported and knew something of our destiny. He also knew he couldn't warn me or do anything to save me. The only reason he was there was to express his love in the way he always had. And that singular moment was one that would stand in my heart always, for it was one of the few times in my life, before or since, that another human being has paid me such honor. I am still humbled by his desperate need just to look at me again, to say with his eyes both "hello" and "good-bye" one last time.

The people in the car gasped as the train jolted into motion. But I might as well have been a statue glued to that little barred window. I watched Nino's eyes until they disappeared into his face. I watched his face until it disappeared into the crowd. I see his tears still.

For the next three weeks, existence became an endless series of alternating plays of oppression. On the one hand, we would be locked in the cars for up to two days without food or fresh water. In that play, life was the semidark interior of a cattle car, with the cries of the hungry and dying accompanied by the increasing stench of our bodies and excrement. On the other hand, we must have stopped a hundred times. Such pauses in our journey of death were made to allow our captors time to eliminate a few more of us by gunshot, and for us to rid the cars of the bodies of those who had died during the previous run. For both reasons, our stops were almost always made in the countryside. We succeeded in littering its beauty with the bodies of our loved ones, thrown along the sidings to rot in the sun.

When we had boarded the train, I saw Cousin Moise struggle to enter a car a few ahead of the one I was in. With a little help, he had hobbled along with us from the headquarters to the port, had managed to survive the boats, and had somehow avoided that bloody wall in Haidary. But he did not survive the train. I can only surmise his end, for I did not see it. Perhaps he died from infection, or perhaps one of the guards finally took notice of his obvious imperfection. Regardless, I am sure that his body was just another one littering some nameless place along the tracks we rode.

If we were fortunate enough to stop by a stream or lake, some of us were permitted to change our water supply. We could go outside at these brief stops, but we were never told exactly when we would be leaving again, and tardiness resulted in a gunshot to the base of the skull. For the most part, we never left the cars, and we were never permitted to remove the straw that we alternately slept and defecated in.

Still, some clung to the belief that life at our destination would be better than we had known in Rhodes. Some believed what we had been told about work and housing in our new location was true. But as the days wore on, as the Nazis piled more and more obscenities on us, their words became hard to believe even for those who clung to belief as an escape from this horrible reality. More and more, we began to believe that what awaited us was more of the same oppression. But no one really knew what translations that oppression would take.

4.

INTO THE ABYSS

OUR LAST STOP seemed like so many others that had preceded it. The lurching of the cars and the sound of the brakes had long since become familiar. Though our senses were dulled from countless hours in the cars, we anticipated another brief respite from their sweltering heat as the doors were opened. Perhaps there would be water at this stop, for raging thirst was our constant companion.

The big door slid open with a grinding groan. Two odd-looking men in dirty striped uniforms quickly moved a set of steps to the opening.

"Schnell! Schnell! Everybody out of the cars! Fall into line here! Hurry! After we check you in we will give you water, food, and a shower." A lean looking soldier had spoken the words, and one of the men in stripes translated them into Spanish. He stood a few feet back from them and held a rifle across his chest.

It was difficult to move after having so little opportunity for physical activity for so long. Grandmama had difficulty even taking a few steps, and Father had to support her once she did. I remember being dizzy when I first stepped toward the door, but I made my way to it quickly. I thought that anything would be an improvement over this stinking cattle box.

The two men stood by the steps, helping us down. One of them, a short, thin man wearing thick spectacles, took me by the forearm as I haltingly negotiated the first step.

"Try to go to the right," he whispered.

"What?"

In the confusion and movement, the other man, the one who had translated the soldier's order, began speaking again in Spanish. But he spoke quietly now and never looked directly at any of us. It was as if he was trying to keep a secret, yet urgently trying to tell all of us something important. It was obvious he was attempting to keep too many words from being heard by the soldier.

"We are Salonik. Jewish from Greece," he whispered. "Give the children to the old people. And don't act like you are sick. Just act like you are healthy, even if you feel terrible. Give the children to the old people. The children have to go. The children have to go. Give them to the old people."

We formed two lines beside the train, one men, the other women. There were many men in stripes scurrying about, either taking our belongings to a large pile near the front of the train or cleaning the straw and debris from the cars. When they thought they would not be heard by the soldiers, they kept telling us to give the children to the old people and to try to go to the right.

Mother looked at Auntie Diana, confused. "What do they mean? Do you understand?"

Auntie Diana clutched Mattie close to her. She didn't say anything to Mother in reply, but her demeanor made it obvious she was not about to give her daughter and little Jaco to Grandmama or anyone. Not in this place.

Our lines were moving quickly, urged along by soldiers with guns and menacing dogs. Here and there, one of the dogs would be released to lunge at someone in the lines, knocking him down, tearing at his groin. Ahead of us, a woman about Auntie Diana's age held a crying baby. One of the guards told her to keep the baby quiet. But she could do little to still the baby's cries. Almost casually, the guard stepped into the line, ripping the baby from her arms.

He turned the now-screaming child upside down, eyeing it curiously as it twisted and cried. In another second, he began pulling its legs apart. With a little jerk, the baby's cries abruptly stopped. As if it were nothing more than a worn-out toy, he then tossed the little body onto the tracks beneath the cars. He turned briefly to the gasping mother, standing in wide-eyed terror.

"This is Auschwitz. Do as you are told."

Within a moment, he had moved down the line, followed closely by another soldier with a dog. The mother, too frightened and shocked to scream, was simply pushed along by the weight of the throng behind her. But I could see her eyes as she constantly turned to look back at the body of her child. They were wide with absolute terror and loss, an indescribable turmoil between preservation and devastation.

I could feel my brief moment of hope drain away from me as if it were just so much urine wetting the straw. I had become numb to the sight and smell of death in the cattle cars. I had become detached from the visions of shootings near the train and the sight of countless bodies strewn in the brush along the right-of-way. But there had still been hope, however fragile, that our lot would improve at our destination.

I realized that I had lied to myself. My numb, conscious mind had calculated that we would be dealt with just as harshly after we reached our destination as before. Yet I ignored my subconscious, desperate hopes and thoughts that things couldn't get any worse than this, that things simply had to get better. I instantly regretted my quiet disdain for those in the car who had dared to express their hope. I realized now that they had been far more in touch with themselves than I, that they had had the courage to speak feelings that I did not.

But just a few feet away from us, hope now lay in a tiny, broken mass beneath the rail car. I dared not look at it. Auntie Diana buried little Mattie's face in her chest, and clutched Jaco to her side. Mother quietly spoke:

"Take care of Stella. Don't leave her. If you go to the other side, we will meet in Italy. We know the language there. Meet in Italy."

I wiped a single tear from my cheek, and found myself at the head of the line.

By the thousands, we wonder what momentary thought, what instantaneous rationale, prompted Dr. Mengele to spare those of us who stood before him. And every second, one of us mourns the millions who never had the opportunity to wonder. He was impeccably dressed as he stood there, deciding our fates. He was a large, broad man with an uncharacteristic warmth to his face. Perhaps it was simply that Stella and I were an even number in his mental count. Perhaps it was that, because of our youth, we appeared vigorous to him. Perhaps it was Stella's shy, childish demeanor as we stood there holding hands. He looked at me, then at her. A small smile crossed his lips, and he pointed casually to the right. In an instant, a decision for life or death had been made, and though we didn't know it, ours had been life.

Similarly, Mother, Grandmama, Auntie Diana, little Mattie and Jaco had no idea that their fate had been death. Within an hour, they would be standing naked in a holding area, waiting to enter what they were told was a shower. Within another hour, they would be standing in the most terrible chamber of horror ever conceived, screaming and crying and praying as they watched the gas form from the crystals on the floor. And later that afternoon, the Sonderkommando would open the chamber to begin removing the bodies, some of them quietly reciting the Kaddish for the thousandth time.

I pray that God was merciful to them. I pray the Sonderkommando found them seated along the wall, having accepted their fate, and having thus died quickly. But I fear for Auntie Diana. I suspect they would have found her among the neat stacks of bodies, among those who tried to escape the gas by climbing atop one another as it rose from the floor. And like so many instances of inhumanity throughout history, the innocent, the most precious, are often those who are exposed to the most suffering. In the chambers, women were often found leaning in those neat piles, still holding their children over their head in a last attempt to spare them the gas. Auntie Diana was a strong woman and a most loving, protective mother.

I looked quickly over my shoulder as they led us away from Mengele. I caught a glimpse of Mother and Grandmama, close together. Mother was looking back in my direction, but I don't know if she really saw me, for there was no expression to say so.

It was to be the last I would ever see her. We never said good-bye.

When I was very young, we would often visit Grandmama. She lived in a house by a huge park, full of trees and grass and children playing in the sun. And there was a window in the living room that opened to that park, a portal between the warmth of Grandmama's smile and the joy of picnics in the grass; a doorway between Mother's embrace and the untethered frolic of children.

In my dreams, I find myself standing in that window to the park. I can feel the cool breeze against my face, and I can smell the freshly cut grass. And in the distance, beneath a tree, Mother and Grandmama laugh with two little girls. I walk to the window to climb through and run to them, but I awaken to today. I awaken to memories of all the days and nights at Grandmama's that were taken away from us.

But there will always be that window in my dreams, until my dreams are no longer dreams.

We were surrounded. This pall of hopelessness was palpable, and we were surrounded. I think that this stark realization of our plight made each of us, in our way, withdraw into the innermost confines of ourselves. As if a switch had been thrown within me, communication with anyone was now based solely on survival. Conversation was a whispered, brief exchange, each participant vying only for leverage in terms of emotional or physical preservation.

This focus made observation difficult. Details of surroundings were limited to those recalled in moments when preservation was in doubt. As such, I don't remember much about having my head shaved, only that it happened. I don't remember much about getting my number tattooed on my arm or that first cold shower, only that it happened. But I do remember the porridge they made us eat that first day. It was a urine-colored, watery mass of rice that smelled like Clorox. Amid the beatings of those who at first refused to eat it, they told us this "medicated" food was intended to cut down on the number of periods we would have. I tried to swallow it without taste. I tried to avoid the smell by breathing through my mouth. As my insides revolted, I resisted the urge to vomit for fear I would be beaten for such an uncontrolled crime. It was, of course, an uncertain choice, but the Germans made it an easy one. I could eat and hope I would not die from this foul smelling gruel, or I could face the consequences of a brutal beating and eat anyway. A woman in front of me fingered the rice into her mouth, trembling in wide-eyed shock as blood trickled down her forehead. I ate every last mouthful.

Shortly after our shower, we were hurried into a large warehouse-like room. Standing naked, we faced piles of clothing that reached to the ceiling, and we were told to quickly find something to wear. Stella and I began rummaging near the bottom of one pile. I had found a pink dress and a pair of shoes that fit fairly well. As I was reaching into the pile to find shoes for Stella, I touched something that felt like hard rubber. I reached in a little further, grasped the object, and pulled.

Stella shrieked. As I pulled it toward me, the clothing fell away to reveal what at first appeared to be a doll. But this doll had eyes that were too real. This doll had hair that was soft. This doll was a stiff little baby, its eyes half open, its mouth parted as if it had died while still suckling. I let go, jumping back to a standing position, staring in blank horror at what now slid down a few inches toward the floor.

Stella's scream brought the fast attention of a guard. She paid no attention to the little body, choosing to ignore it as if it were, indeed, but a doll.

"Schnell, schnell!" She picked up a pair of sandals, thrusting them at my sister as if they were brass knuckles aimed at her stomach. "Form a line by the door now! Schnell!"

I was strangely relieved that Stella had been so frightened, for her terror permitted me to defer my attention from the gruesome reality I had just revealed. I put my arm around her as we hurried toward the line. I tried to quiet her shuddering, wide-eyed whimpers, focusing my fear on avoiding more attention from the guards. Like so many horrible moments endured in Auschwitz-Birkenau, I shut it out from that instant of recognition until years later, when my subconscious jolted me from sleep, that little gray face still drifting before my eyes.

I suppose that for those of us who were there, it is this continued suffering that is the most damning aspect of being a "survivor." The world may have breathed a collective sigh of relief upon our liberation, but there is no liberation from what we endured. There are only days of escape from our memories. There are only days when each of us happens to be strong enough to suppress the ghastliness of the Holocaust experience. But we are human, and fallible, even unto ourselves. There are nights when those memories break through from the subconscious. There are nights when we awaken, drenched in sweat, with a picture or two released from our individually locked-up storehouses of horror. They are pictures that each of us wishes every day had never been taken. They are pictures we hope in futility we can forget. But they are pictures that must never be forgotten by a world with too short a memory.

But for now, it was as if my encounter with the baby had never happened. There were, after all, more important things to deal with. There was my emotional survival, linked irrevocably by my mother's words with Stella. There was my physical survival, tied now to the avoidance of attention. Without realizing it, my existence, and that of those I shared incarceration with, was simply a matter of staying alive and aware from one day to the next, and of somehow enduring each day's moments of horror without losing one's sanity.

Our new home was in Lager A, a group of barracks in the Birkenau camp adjacent to Auschwitz. We were put in Barrack 20. It was a long building, with three-tiered bunks along both walls. Stella and I shared the bottom level with other girls from Rhodes: Matti, Lucia, and Sara. We also shared one blanket among the five of us.

At the end of Barrack 20 were a few small rooms, occupied by the Blockovas. They were army prisoners, some of whom had been there for years, who collaborated with the camp authorities and assisted significantly in maintaining control over the rest of us. Some of the Blockovas were sometimes gentle and understanding people. Most of the Blockovas most times were as brutal and sadistic as any of the SS. Helenca was the chief Blockova in Barrack 20. She was a tall Polish woman who ruled the barrack with a cruel combination of contempt, intimidation, and beatings. For her efforts in supporting the camp organization and its hierarchy of death, she was afforded better food than the rest of us and usually her own room in the barrack.

But there were other prices to be paid, even by the Blockovas. For while they were afforded a degree of privacy unlike the rest of us, they frequently had to share it with the Germans. Such matters were not a matter of choice for them. They were just another tool in the struggle to survive just another day. They were an accepted medium of exchange for a small favor or payment of a bartered debt.

Any sort of passion, let alone love, of course, was out of the question here. Sex was simply a bodily function reserved for those who could afford it. Though the general barrack population sometimes bartered or was clever enough to obtain a brief encounter in the latrine, sex between the Blockovas and Germans was a much more frequent event. It was another price to be paid to preserve one's position and, hence, survival in the Birkenau community.

But we had no position. We were below the first rung of the Birkenau ladder. We were nothing. We huddled together to stay warm that first night in the bottom bunk. There were no words spoken, not even a whisper. We just lay there in the dim light, seeing dully the glistening hopelessness of a hundred open eyes.

Matti began to scream. Nothing had happened to her, and no one

had spoken to her. She just began to scream and struggle to get out
of the bunk. Sara tried to hold her, and Lucia, fearing the attention
of the Blockovas, held her hand over her mouth to try to quiet her.
But Matti persevered. Screaming again and again, she struggled free
of us, climbing over Stella and me as she left the bunk. She immediately ran in circles, screaming and muttering meaningless words
almost too rapidly to be understood. And then she fell to the floor.

I don't know why Matti died that evening, but I do know how.
There is, I believe, an inseparable link between the emotions and
the physical being. In Matti's case, the emotional part of her had
been overwhelmed by the day's events. Who knows what family
members she had said good-bye to that day? Who knows what sub-
jugated horrors she had seen on the train? Who knows what brutal
events she had been subjected to? Perhaps she had encountered a
vision too horrific to control. Perhaps she had some long-untreated
malady none of us knew about. It didn't matter. Within a few
minutes, the Blockovas came and took her away. I said the Kaddish
for her, never moving from my place on the bunk and never uttering
a word of it aloud. For tonight at least, there would be a little more
room under our blanket.

They would wake us with whistles at 4:00 a.m. "Auschten, auschten! Up! Up!" Helenca would shout. At times, the Nazis would
walk through the barrack, inspecting us as they passed through. More
commonly, we would be made to stand outside, sometimes for hours,
until such time as they deemed fit to count us and review our fitness
for work. They always seemed to have such steely, blue, uncaring
eyes. After the first day, I was afraid to look in them. I was afraid to
be recognized for having any kind of emotion. I only wanted to be
inconspicuous, to look down and to pass the morning inspection without incident. For I knew the fate of those who did not. Their survival
was limited to hours or less. Sometimes they were shot on the spot.
Sometimes they were taken elsewhere to be beaten to death. Sometimes they were taken to the infirmary, where an injection of phenol
to the heart ended life very quickly.

We learned that death was an ever-present companion to all of us.
Death could be a saviour, a merciful, quick escape. Death could also
be a cruel prankster, an unmerciful reaper who waited for his moment
just around the corner from your consciousness. You might hear the
gunshot, see the body of a friend slump to the mud, or just realize
one day that someone was no longer around you. When you did,

Death would turn to look at you. He would stare at you with anticipation.

Despite being sick from the long train ride to Birkenau, Auntie Fortune had somehow managed to be selected for life by Dr. Mengele. She was in Barrack 20 with the rest of us and had managed to suffer through those first few days, I think, because her quiet, reserved nature allowed her to merge easily into that sea of humbled faces. But her sickness worsened quickly, and before most of us knew what going to the infirmary really meant, she asked to be checked in for care of her malady. Of course, she never came back. As the whispers about the gas and the infirmary and all the other ways to die reached us, I realized that Death had likely found his time with Auntie Fortune. I realized how close he'd been to me. I realized he could be waiting for any of us before we even knew it.

Those first few weeks Stella and I carried bricks. I don't know what part of the camp we were marched to, and I don't know what project we were working on. But I carried red bricks. I have since heard that they were building yet another crematorium during the time I was there, but I don't know for sure. I just know there were countless hundreds of bricks for countless hours.

By evening, we would be led back to Barrack 20 for dinner. Our evening meal consisted of watered soup, sometimes with turnips in it, sometimes with little more than the water itself. Other Jews would serve it to us from huge cauldrons, ladling it into the metal cups we had been given for food.

I hated turnips. I hated them before Birkenau, and I hate them even more now. But survival was everything, and after a very few days in the camps, the smallest bit of food could mean existing for another day. When we weren't being watched, I would always try to make myself presentable to the servers, especially if there were men among them. I would smile and whisper words of encouragement, all designed to obtain perhaps an extra piece of turnip in my soup, or if we were lucky enough to have it, an extra piece of bread to share with Stella. But at Birkenau, survival depended so much on chance. In this Godless place, chance took over for God. If I happened to be in the right place in line at the right time with the right smile, I might get that extra piece of turnip. But other times, the Nazis might be watching when I passed, and I would get only water.

After dinner we had free time, if it could be called that. Once we learned "the way things worked" in Birkenau, we understood that we could sometimes wander about the immediate confines of the barrack, particularly if the Blockovas were in a mood to look the other way or were otherwise indisposed. That meant that sometimes, either after dinner or in the morning before counting, we were relatively free to walk about the Lager and the immediate confines of its fenced yard, which bordered the men's camp. It was along this fence that I first saw Father, Uncle Rahamin, Jaco, and Salvo.

Father immediately began crying when he saw Stella and me. "Are you OK, Laura? Is Stella all right?"

"We're still here, Papa. We're OK so far."

"I miss Mother so much."

His words struck me hard, because he didn't ask where Mother was. I didn't know where she was, and I was afraid to ask if he knew.

In retrospect, I believe he did. We stood only a few feet apart, and the look in his eyes was like nothing I had ever seen. He kept repeating "I miss mother so much" over and over again, as if he knew with certainty her fate. And he seemed but a crestfallen shell of what little had been left since we departed Rhodes. While most of us had at least a hope of survival, it seemed as if he had none. It was as if some irreplaceable part of him had been forever stripped away.

Did he know? And if he knew, how?

I can only surmise that there is a communication that sometimes exists beyond that which is spoken and beyond that conveyed by touch. I believe that Father sensed her death and believed in himself enough to know the truth. How strange the things love teaches us, and in such strange places!

We stood but a few feet apart, separated by the wire, and for a few moments fed each other hope. There were words of love and encouragement, accompanied by frequent looks over the shoulder to check on the attention, if any, of the Blockovas. A sudden, loud snapping sound came from my left, followed quickly by a strange, sweet burnt smell. We looked in the direction of the sound almost as quickly as it happened. A young girl, probably no older than I, had tried to pass a piece of bread beneath the wire to her father. She had doubtless done it many times, for her wasted appearance belied the fact that she had been here longer than the rest of us.

But the God of Chance had forsaken her. As she lay prone and began passing the bread beneath the wire, her hand grazed the bottom-most strand. She had been electrocuted instantly, the current burning its way up her arm and into her body.

We were learning the Birkenau way quickly. After the initial horror of seeing her die before us, we all looked about for the Blockovas and guards. Seeing that they paid no attention, we went on with our whispered conversations. No one tried to pull the girl from where she lay. No one even tried to check to see if she was somehow still alive. A few of the men across the wire crowded around her father, who was wailing in despair. But the rest of us buried the incident in our subconscious and went on with the business of survival. Did we care? Of course we did. Did we have the luxury? Not for more than a moment.

Stella and I tried to see the men at the fence every day after that, usually in the early morning before the counting. Sometimes we didn't get the opportunity, because either the men were working at another location or we were. And sometimes there was a selection, the most feared word in our Birkenau vocabulary. It was simple, really. They would line us up outside or inside the barrack and "select" those who appeared weak or sick or even looked a little different. To be selected, of course, meant death. Death by the gas, death by gunshot, death through a visit to the infirmary, death by any of a hundred other means.

Sometimes only Father, or Uncle Rahamin, or Jaco and Salvo were there to meet us across the wire. Such meetings, or lack thereof, quickly began to define the quality of our day. If all the men were there and we had some time to talk, my day was at least tolerable, for there was at least hope. If no one was there or if Stella and I couldn't be, we would spend the day wondering if the men were all right, wondering where they were, wondering if someone had been selected for the gas.

At least there were no more pretenses here in Birkenau. Inside the wire, there was no need to lie. Though no one spoke of it much, the SS made it quite clear what your fate would be if you were selected, if you disobeyed the rules conjured up for the moment, if you didn't work hard enough. You would be taken to the gas. You would die. And if they finally broke your spirit, if you ran about the camps screaming, if you ran purposely into the wire as many girls did, so much the better. You were one less mouth to feed, one less body to watch, and no one even had to go to the trouble of shooting you.

If you survived longer than a few days, the threat of death was not a threat at all. The threat of how you would die and how long it would take, was. Once the decision was made, they could be merciful and just shoot you. Conversely, they could send you to the infirmary and make you wait for hours, knowing full well your destination was Dr. Mengele's needle in your heart. And there were other ways to die, more gruesome and more prolonged. With complete disdain, the Germans would use these as a demonstrated means of control.

Shortly after we had arrived in Barrack 20, they asked us if anyone in our group was pregnant. I remember a young, beautiful woman stepped forward, her abdomen barely showing her condition. They told her to come to the infirmary for special treatment to ensure the success of her pregnancy and protect the baby. With only a little reluctance, she followed them out of the barrack.

A few days later we returned from work, and the young woman was lying in the bunk across from mine. Most of her body was covered with black, blue, and red bruises. This beating had preceded the removal of her fetus, which had been done without anesthetic. A huge, festering wound across her abdomen stained her smock in a foul-smelling rainbow of yellow, green, and dark red. And she was alive. She told us of how they had beaten and whipped her for having the audacity to be pregnant. She told us of seeing the knife puncture her abdomen, of screaming and being beaten about the head. She died on that bunk within an hour.

There was no reason to torture and murder an innocent woman and her unborn child, but reason did not exist here. There was absolutely no reason to bring the woman back to Barrack 20, save one. It was to deliver a message to all of us: That you would die was unimportant. How you would die depended on your obedience and the only God in Birkenau, the God of Chance.

We spent the night with the young woman's body. By the time we returned from work the next day, someone had removed all trace of her.

Each day still alive was a minor victory, but they passed from one to the next with imperceptible slowness. Counting them was unimportant, and we quickly lost track of time. The only measure of the clock was sunrise and sunset and being alive yet another day.

But there were many selections. One morning I approached the fence, and Jaco was waiting for me.

"Where's Father?"

Jaco pursed his lips. "Oh, he went to work. He'll be back."

My entire body went limp, but somehow I stood. I knew he was lying. "No. Tell me the truth, Jaco. Where's Father?"

Uncle Rahamin came up to Jaco. There were tears in his eyes.

I looked at Jaco. I looked at Uncle Rahamin. I knew, but I still asked the question. "Where's Father?"

"Laura, his last words were, 'Take care of my children.' I will, Laura. Somehow I will. I promised him. I will take care of you and Stella and your brothers. I will. I promise."

So it was I learned that Father had been chosen to be an actor in this play of death. I turned away from the fence, struggling to bury this most personal tragedy as I had buried so many others. I had no idea where my mother was, but I guessed she was dead. I now knew with certainty my father's fate. How many more would there be? How long would it be before it was my turn? How would I continue these daily struggles to survive with fewer and fewer reasons to?

I cried a long cry, but shed few tears. I cried again when I found a way to tell Stella that Father was gone, but shed no tears. I knew they had taken my father to the gas. To this day, my biggest hope is that his wait at the chamber was a short one. He had given me life, had given me protection, had given me so much of himself. I had so little to give back, save a renewed desire to survive this hell. To do that, I had to bury him so quickly. I never even said a prayer for him. I no longer believed God was listening, if He existed at all.

I had been in Birkenau not quite a month. Once a week, we were herded to a special barrack to shower. There were no stalls in the building, nor was there soap, shampoo, or hot water. Just shower spigots along the walls. We took off our clothes outside the barrack, went in and showered for a few minutes, then came back out and put our clothes on. There were no towels, and as August had given way to mid-September, the weather had begun to turn colder.

Epidemics of typhus, dysentery, influenza, and a host of other maladies were common in the camps, and the showers served as little more than an encouragement for the contraction of such diseases. Though I will never be certain, the showers and lack of the ability to dry off may have played a role in the development of two abscesses on my legs. They probably began as abrasions that, due to the lack of sanitation, became infected.

Fortunately, they were about mid-thigh, slightly above the hemline of the little pink dress I had been wearing since August. At first I ignored them, hoping they would simply heal. But as they continued to fester and become worse, hiding them from the eyes of the Blockovas became increasingly difficult.

At the same time, many of us were killed because of the cold. By early October, snow had come to Birkenau. A littering of white among our muddy tracks about the Lager at first, it seemed that scarcely a week passed before there were several inches of snow.

Of course, we all were made to stand selections and our days were spent carrying bricks in the cold. Some of the girls in Barrack 20 had the idea of ripping our blankets into large strips, which were then worn as something of an undergarment across our chests as a means to stay warm. It was only a day or so before we all were wearing our blankets.

But the Blockovas soon found out about our invention. It was treason to rip blankets, they told us, and insisted during a selection that we tell them who the perpetrators were. No one spoke, and no one came forward to admit her guilt.

It was our only small victory in Birkenau, but the price of that achievement was high. If no one would admit guilt, then we all had to pay. That morning we were made to kneel in the snow and, as long as no one would talk, every morning thereafter. For hours every morning, we knelt. For all the days they made us suffer so, no one spoke.

It didn't matter any more. After the first day, frostbite struck many of us. After the second day, two girls dropped dead in the snow. After the third, another few died. But it was worth it, for we were quietly demonstrating a solidarity that none of us thought we could. I think I realized there in the snow that death could be a weapon, and in this place, it was the only weapon we had. With each one of us who dropped sadly in the snow, the will of those remaining became stronger. Before too many more days passed, the Blockovas came to understand that their ploy was fast resulting in the exact opposite of their intent. No one spoke. No one betrayed the inventors of our blankets-turned-underwear. Our punishment ended when we were abruptly moved to Barrack 7. Life was much the same in our new home, but the Blockovas in charge seemed somewhat kinder to us for the most part. We had won, though a quarter of us had died for the victory.

The incident had helped me ignore the sores on my legs, but the cold had done nothing to help heal them. After only a few days in Barrack 7, I began to realize I had no choice. There was something wrong with me, yet notice of my affliction would mean a sure ticket to the infirmary and Dr. Mengele. I did my best to hide the abscesses and my increasing fear.

But my affliction became worse and worse. The sores had become red and blue in color and protruded about an inch from my thigh. Walking became very painful, and by late October, I realized I could not hide the problem much longer. A trip to the infirmary was as certain as I now believed discovery of my malady was imminent. The Nazis could almost smell illness and plucked those who were sick like overripe apples for baking in the crematorium.

Despite the cold, I went outside one night to be alone. I was terrified. I wanted to live, even with so few reasons to. I wanted to survive, but survival at that moment seemed very remote. Despite my terror, I clung to strands of hope in pure desperation. Perhaps the planes that now seemed to bomb almost nightly would bomb us and I could escape to find help. Perhaps we would have a few days of dry weather and my wounds would begin to heal. I rounded the corner of the barrack, and hope became reality.

Another girl was sitting alone, leaning against the barrack wall. She was pale and thin, and I noticed that blonde hair had begun to grow back on her shaved head. She was wearing a heavy coat to stay warm, a coat I wished for in the cold. But she seemed incapable of smiling. She looked forlorn, her pale blue eyes reminding me somewhat of the uncaring eyes of the Nazis.

She hadn't heard me round the corner of the barrack and didn't notice me until, with a start, she recognized another human was standing a few feet away. But I said nothing to her. I simply sat a couple yards away, leaning against the wall as she was. I was in so much pain. I didn't want to talk to anyone.

But she spoke to me in a language I didn't understand. With some apprehension, I replied to her in Italian that I was Italian and didn't know her language. In broken Italian, she spoke back to me.

"I am from Russia. My name is Marushka. What is yours?"

"Laura."

She paused, eyeing me carefully. Quite suddenly, her expression took on a dreamy, peaceful look. "You remind me of my cousin, Laura. You look just like her." She kept staring at me as she spoke, but her gaze did not make me uncomfortable. It was as if she had suddenly found someone she had not seen for a very long time. I didn't mind playing the role. It took my mind away from my own problem.

"You are Jewish, Laura?"

"Yes. And you?"

Marushka paused, still staring intently at me. "I am not Jewish. I am a political prisoner. Have you heard of the city of Moscow?"

"Of course."

"I am from Moscow." She paused again, eyeing me carefully, then moved the few feet to where I sat. "You are sick? You don't feel well?" It was almost as much a statement as a question. Perhaps she somehow saw my pain. More likely she saw my terror.

Reluctantly, I pulled up the hem of the little pink dress, revealing my sores. "I'm scared they will find these, Marushka. Please. Please don't tell anyone."

She touched my leg to examine the sores more closely. Her touch was cold, but extremely gentle. It was as if there was a sudden understanding between us. An almost instantaneous knowledge, with that touch, of the suffering we shared, each in our own way.

"I think I can take care of that, Laura. Hide your wounds as best you can until tomorrow, and meet me here tomorrow night. I will bring something that may work to heal you."

"What?"

She looked askance, as if making sure no one was within earshot. "I will bring you honey and flour. I know prisoners who will give it to me from the kitchen." She touched my arm. "Listen, Laura. You mix the flour and honey and put it on your sores like a poultice. Then you cover it with a piece of cloth to keep it warm so it will heal."

She looked directly in my eyes, as if giving the most important part of the instruction. "You do this every day for a week, Laura. You change the poultice every day." She paused. "If this does not work, you will have to go to the infirmary."

I began to cry, but she again touched my arm. "Don't worry, Laura. There is no point in worry. You come here tomorrow night and I will bring the flour and honey."

And with that, she was gone. She disappeared so quickly, it was almost as if she was an angel who had come only to help me. I put my face in my arms and wept.

I came to see Marushka almost every day. She would always be sitting in that same place, up against the barrack wall, and it seemed she always managed to bring something to make my existence tolerable. Sometimes it was a piece of cheese or bread she had obtained from her friends in the kitchen. Sometimes it was a piece of blanket or other cloth that Stella or I would put under our clothes to keep warm. Sometimes it was just a smile. It didn't matter. Marushka had been my angel of deliverance that first night. That she would be more than a momentary blessing was God's way, I think, of healing that part of me beyond my sores.

Until the sores appeared, I had been able to push myself into that same locked away place I'd found on the boats. Existence consisted of taking care of Stella, of making sure she was all right. Consciousness consisted of surviving what occurred each day, each hour, each minute. I had pushed so much into that locked away place.

But when the sores appeared, my strategy began to fail. The doors, bulging with the pressure of so much horror, had begun to creep open like those squealing cattle car doors. My sores had forced me to become aware of myself. As long as they existed, I could no longer fully detach myself from the daily atrocities I witnessed. My whimpering that first night with Marushka had not been driven by fear of selection or the gas; it was an overriding terror that the doors would burst open, that I would be buried in a sea of horror, that I would run in circles, as Matti had, and fall dead.

I will never know if Marushka knew how much more of me she saved than just my life. As the days wore on, her concoction of honey and flour brought my sores to a head, and they finally began to heal. Reluctantly, I accepted those bits of food and warmth Marushka brought, but not before insisting at times that she at least share the food. She was so thin and gaunt. Like the angel she was to my spirit, it seemed as if the slightest wind would simply whisk her away from me. And I feared that. I feared that she would disappear before I had had time to heal completely.

We talked of so many things. She of her family and home. Me, little by little, of the brutality, the torture, the atrocities of this place. It trickled from beneath those doors, and Marushka soaked it up, took it away. I could talk to her. I could cry with her, in little sobs not loud enough to be heard. I remember one night it had begun to snow, and she put her arm around me, huddling close so that the both of us might stay a little warm. I remember looking inside myself, and the doors no longer bulged and groaned with the weight of so much misery.

"Laura? Why do you cry tonight?"

I looked down. My tears had made little dark splotches on my dress. They had filled my eyes, dribbled down my cheeks, but I hadn't noticed until Marushka spoke. I looked in her eyes.

"Because I have you."

She stared back at me gently, but I could see a look of alarm cross her eyes. "No, Laura, you do not have me. You only have this moment with me." She looked away, and I could tell that dreamy countenance once again came over her.

"Do not make the mistake of relying on anyone, Laura. No matter how much they love you. Existence here is too precarious. I might be gone tomorrow."

Her arm tightened a little around me, but she still stared off in the distance. "Take what someone gives you, Laura, but don't dare hope they'll be here to give to you again tomorrow. It can destroy you faster than the gas."

"I know, Marushka. I know that. You have taught me that." I took a deep breath. "But I will have you always in my heart. No matter what happens to either of us, I will always have you here."

I smiled, a tiny, closed-mouth expression. It felt so strange.

Winter had finally covered our muddy tracks with snow. I noticed that Marushka was beginning to slip back into what seemed to be a continuous depression. The fog of sadness that I had felt that first night with her once again appeared to envelop her, and she became more withdrawn. Our conversations strayed away from what confronted us and began to wander into our dreams. Marushka had so many dreams. She would talk to me of the solidarity movement in Russia, of the philosophy of equality embraced by the group she had been a part of. She wanted to go to school to become a chemical engineer. She wanted to marry and raise a family. She missed her mother and father so much and wondered if they were alive. She hoped against hope that she would have the chance to find out.

I trudged through the half-frozen mud around the corner of Barrack 7. Wind blew a wet snow about my field of vision. And Marushka wasn't there. For a week or so I slipped out to meet her every night, but Marushka wasn't there. In November, a hard winter storm blew in. I stopped looking for her. It was too cold.

Perhaps, on a whim, the Blockovas had murdered her for wearing strips of blanket under her clothes as we had. Perhaps she had been selected. Perhaps she had met her end in a hundred other ways so common in this hell. But for me, Marushka never died. For me, she is as alive as the first moment I saw her. I sometimes light candles for Father and Mother, for Auntie Diana and Grandmama, for all my family lost in those days. Among those flickering lights, there is always a flame for Marushka.

My days wore on. With each one, there were more red bricks to carry, more shivering in that little pink dress, more turnip soup. The nights were just as slow and cold. There was no heat in Barrack 7, and the blanket we shared among us gave little protection against the cold. I would lie there awake, feeling the mist from my breath without seeing it, listening to the groans and misery of those around me. I was so alone, but so too was everyone. Somehow I found solace in that I was not alone in my aloneness.

And then I would hear it. A low humming, quiet at first, no louder than the sleeping moans from the bunks around me. But it became louder, soon breaking through that sleeping background into its own distinctive sound. The planes. I would listen to their approach and the sounds of distant antiaircraft batteries. I would hear the muffled rumbles of the bombs. They reminded me of Izguro, but I prayed they would fall on me, prayed they would throw me to the floor as I had been thrown to the ground that night on the way to the air raid shelter. I prayed they would blast this insidious place to dust.

Sometimes the barrack would quake a little when the target was close or when a few bombs missed their mark. But they never bombed us. The rumbles and little quakes would fade away quickly, and the drone of the planes crossed the night to silence. The silence after the bombings brought with it a feeling of entrapment, of utter abandonment. Did they know we were here? Did they care? Did anyone in the world wonder what had happened to us?

Today I know they knew we were there. That the Allies couldn't spare a few bombs to try to end such misery is as much an atrocity as any we faced. Instead, they used us, just like the Germans used our energies to build more tools of war. Bombing runs near Auschwitz began with the bombardier sighting on the crematorium smokestacks, to obtain bearings for bomb drops on the nearby munitions factories.

Still, emotions were a means to survival, for without them, there was no reason to exist. Whether the moments of hope brought by the sound of the planes or the utter despair at their departure, at least there was something to feel. Good or bad feelings mattered far less than feeling anything at all.

Stella and I lived for each other now. While we were not particularly close at home in Rhodes due to our differences in age and personality, here we clung to each other. We were, as far as we knew, practically all that was left of that large circle of love we had both grown up with, that close warmth and caring known as family. Mother's last words to me kept repeating themselves every time I looked at Stella. We were doing the best we could to honor her instructions. We were surviving.

If you'd been there long enough, you learned there were ways that, with a certain degree of risk, you might be able to obtain an extra bit of clothing or a little food. Mine was the discovery of the waste bin next to the barrack where they prepared food for the Blockovas. For some time, I had made regular, secretive trips to the spot to collect potato peels. I would stuff as many of the filthy strips in my mouth as possible, then carry several more back to the barrack for Stella to eat.

Of course, there was always the risk of death for such a transgression. When my moment came, I was fortunate enough to remember that Marushka had told me to run if I was confronted by a Blockova or guard. I might be shot only a few steps from where the incident occurred, she said, but at least I would give myself a chance at surviving.

So it was I was hunched over, picking potato peels off the ground and stuffing them in my mouth. I had forgotten to look around for danger in the last few seconds and paid the price when the stinging shock of a rifle butt to my shoulder splattered me to the ground. But I remembered Marushka's words. Wincing in pain I scrambled and ran toward the corner of the barrack and kept running until I reached the relative safety of Barrack 7.

I never did see who had hit me. I had simply run away, and perhaps the person had not wanted to waste a bullet. Whatever the reason I was allowed to live, it would be a long time until hunger became severe enough to drive me to again scavenge for potato peels. Stella and I would be a little hungrier for a while, but at least we were alive.

Still, I began to notice that Stella was looking progressively more tired and worn than usual. She was only 13 and had always been somewhat slender. But like the rest of us, she had lost considerable weight. She now appeared painfully thin. I decided that perhaps some fresh air would be good for both of us, and we trudged through the mud and snow, around the corner of Barrack 7, to where Marushka and I had so often sat and talked. But just as Marushka had always seemed pale, so Stella now appeared flushed and red. I put my hand to her forehead. I opened the top of her dress, unfastening the first few buttons. She was red everywhere I looked, and she was burning with fever.

I instantly became panicky. How could I not have noticed Stella's sickness until now? What was wrong with her? What was wrong with me? What would Mother say if we did not both survive? My heart raced. Stella was sick! She was all I knew I had left of my immediate family and she was sick! What could I possibly do to save her? Where could I go for help? Stella began to tremble. She sensed she was not well and seeing my panic, she began to cry.

I did the only thing I could do. There was no Marushka now with a poultice of honey and flour. There was no Mother to tell me what was wrong, and no Father to take us to the doctor. There was only the Blockovas. I took Stella inside the barrack, put her in our bunk, and went to the Blockova's room.

I stood outside her door, which was open. Noticing me and what I'm sure was my look of terror, she came out of the room and asked me what was wrong.

"My sister Stella is sick. She is red all over and has a fever. Can you help her?"

She crossed her arms as she stared down at me. She was a large woman, about 30, and a little overweight. And though I feared her as much as I feared anyone in authority, she had always seemed a little less brutal than the other Blockovas. She seemed somehow to have a streak of humanness about her. At least the few times she had spoken to me, she spoke as if I was a human being, and this was no exception.

"There is an epidemic. You should take your sister to the infirmary."

I feared this would be the Blockova's response, and I could not accept it. The infirmary meant death. The only person I had known who had ever come back from the infirmary was the pregnant woman, butchered and dying.

"I can't send her there!" I stammered. "I'll never see her again!"

Stella was sitting on the bunk I had taken her to. She was close enough to us to hear the conversation, and at mention of the infirmary, she began to cry again. She knew as well as the rest of us that a trip there was, for all practical purposes, a death sentence.

The Blockova shifted her feet impatiently, but a small look of compassion crossed her face. Unfolding her arms, she held her hands out plaintively.

"Look. Your sister will not pass a selection in the condition she is in. You have no choice. She is sick. You must send her to the infirmary. You might spare her today, but tomorrow, if you do nothing, she will find the gas."

She turned away from me. "There is nothing I can do. Take her to the infirmary." She closed the door as she reentered her room.

Stella was crying desperately. "Don't make me go to the infirmary, Laura! Don't make me go." She sobbed. "I can get better, Laura. There haven't been any selections for a while. I can get better. Don't make me go!"

I swallowed hard. "You have to go, Stella. There have been no selections for a while. There could be one tomorrow!" I took her hand. "Listen to me. I want you to go to the infirmary. It is our only chance. You go there and I will come every day and knock on the outside of the wall where you are. I promise, Stella. Even if I have to die, I will stay here for you. I will come and knock every day. If there is a selection, I will hide from it and I will come and knock on the wall. I promise."

Stella continued pleading with me not to go, but eventually she acquiesced. We walked slowly to the infirmary, hand in hand. I had no idea if my decision had been the right one. I had no idea if I would ever see my sister again.

Stella wept quietly as we entered the infirmary. A Jewish nurse, sitting at a small desk just inside the door, rose as we entered. She was young, with dark hair confirming the fact that she had survived long enough for it to grow out a few inches. But her demeanor portrayed her strategy. She was distant, never seeming to look directly at either of us or anyone else around her. Her posture was humble and quiet.

"My sister Stella is sick."

The nurse looked Stella up and down briefly, but never looked in her eyes.

"Come with me. You can go now." She took Stella, still weeping, behind another set of doors and into the sick bay. I didn't leave, risking notice until she returned a few minutes later.

"Please. Please tell me where my sister is. I promised her I would knock outside every day."

The nurse didn't look at me, but simply sat back at her desk. "You should not be here. You must go now. You must leave."

I realized there was no point in trying to argue with the nurse. She would not tell me where Stella was in the infirmary. She would not tell me anything. Perhaps she was trying to protect herself. Perhaps she was wary of giving the only answer she could give truthfully— that most people who went to the infirmary would never return. It didn't matter. I turned and, still hearing Stella's cries in my mind, walked out of the infirmary toward Barrack 7.

There was confusion and more motion than normal as I approached the barrack. People were scurrying about, as much as living skeletons could scurry. Still, I didn't realize what was happening. I only thought of Stella and how I might find a way to find where she was in the infirmary.

"Raus! Raus!" ("Out! Out!")

The words hit me like a hammer. A selection! The Nazis and the Blockovas were rounding up everyone in Barrack 7, making them come outside and line up. Old and young, healthy and sick, the women were slowly coming out into the cold. Some of them couldn't even walk, but still they were driven out into the snow.

I panicked. My mind raced with thoughts of Stella and thoughts of death and thoughts of Nazis. I ran into the barrack, shoving my way past those who were coming out. I found myself again at the Blockova's room.

"I have to stay! I have to stay! I have to see my sister in the infirmary. Please! Please hide me from the selection! I have to see my sister!"

I might as well have asked the Blockova to free me. I might as well have asked her to sign her own warrant for the gas. But I was desperate, and perhaps a little insane with the potential of not obeying my mother's last wish.

By all rights she should have hit me. She should have taken me to the Nazis right away. But she just looked at me sadly.

"There is no place to hide here. You know that. If you try to hide, they will find you and you will be shot." She shook her head. "There is no place to hide."

My breath came in quick, convulsive bursts. I stood before her, trembling. "It's all right if I am shot. It's all right! I promised Stella. I promised my mother!"

"There is no place to hide here." She turned and walked away.

How strange the ways of chance and the ways this strange god worked in Birkenau. Of all the beasts of terror I had faced, there was one, that one Blockova, who was still a human being. By chance, she had been there the day that I had noticed Stella's sickness. By chance, I had gone to her room. By chance, she had not had me killed for asking to be hidden. By chance, there had been no Nazis near when I spoke to her. I would never have taken Stella to the infirmary had she not insisted it was my only option. There is no doubt in my mind that Stella would have been sent to the gas that very day had I not taken her to the Jewish nurse. By chance, a selection was being held, and by chance, Stella had escaped it by less than an hour. The question now was, would I?

Mengele stood at the head of the line outside of Barrack 7. I wondered if I would once again be given a chance to live. I wondered if the God of Chance was still working in my favor or if my chances had run out.

I remember stumbling into line, thinking how fortunate it was that Mengele was here and not in the infirmary with Stella. I remember seeing the girls who had been selected, led off to a small area just inside another barrack. Stella would have been with them, I thought. Surely, Mengele would have seen her plight, would have seen her sickness, would have condemned her on the spot.

But I, too, must now have taken on the look of the dead. My chance to keep my last promise to Mother had been stripped away from me. Though my sores, thanks to Marushka, had healed, I had lost considerable weight since being incarcerated, and my little pink dress, still hanging limply on my shoulders, was in tatters. I took a deep breath as I passed him and remember thinking I should somehow put some sparkle in my eyes. But ever since that last day in Rhodes, my world had turned from blue-skied innocence to the gray of brutal experience. And now, as I stood there briefly, the chill of dark winter's death blew through me. I shivered, and hoped immediately it hadn't shown. I swallowed a hard, dry swallow and found myself once again with the living. I had passed the selection.

It seemed as if my vision of existence had become somehow blurred. All the time I had been in Birkenau, I had usually been able to bury the atrocities I witnessed and maintain a keen awareness of myself. It was, after all, a fundamental part of survival here. But it all became fuzzy now. It all began to spin.

By late afternoon I found myself with a small group of girls I didn't know. We were being led into Auschwitz, and I had no idea why we were being taken there or how I had been placed in that group. My mind was filled with thoughts of Stella and thoughts of lost hope. How foolish I had been! I had been able to survive in this place of hopelessness by not relying on anyone. Marushka had been right. To rely on anyone meant you had trust in them. And if you had trust, you had hope. To have hope in Birkenau was to waste your energies. I had lied to myself. I had prided myself on self-reliance, without ever stopping to realize how much I relied on Stella. I relied on the promise I had made to Mother on her behalf. I relied on that promise because it gave me hope that I would survive. I would expend my last breath protecting Stella, for in giving her life, I had been giving myself hope. But now hope had been placed in the infirmary, and I found myself awash in that blurry sea of despair. Like a filthy tide, we were poured into a room, told to remove our clothes, and were locked inside.

It was very dim and cool, like the basement of a huge building. The room was large, with a flat cement floor where we stood and a series of small steps that seemed to lead to nowhere. Everything was painted white, save for a huge red tank that stood in one corner near us.

"What is this place?" one of the girls asked.

I turned toward her numbly. I wasn't sure she had spoken to me. "What is this place?" she repeated, seeming to ask the question of anyone who might answer. "Why are we here?"

For a moment, I regained some sort of cognizance. Perhaps it was that she was small and dark, like Stella. Perhaps it was that despite her short black hair and the dirt that clung to all of us, she was stunningly beautiful. I looked in her eyes. It had been the first time I had looked in anyone's eyes for months.

"I don't know," I whispered a response to her questions. We always whispered, whether anyone was near or not.

We found ourselves sitting on the stairs, huddling together to stay a little warm. The girl was leaning against me, as if to somehow draw strength from what little I had. Slowly, I fell back into my blurred trance. Slowly, I began to escape the sinister feel of this place. I thought again of Stella and wondered if she was alive. My world began to spin again, in that slow whirlpool of nothingness. The floor was cold. The tank gurgled and groaned in the dim light. The door opened.

A handful of our tormentors entered the room. I stood slowly in response to their shouts and laughter, but something was strangely wrong. These men were laughing! A few of them were in the Nazi uniforms I had come to hate, those strange uniforms that undoubtedly the gypsy had seen in her cards. But they did not have their usual trim appearance. They were somehow disheveled, somehow wrinkled and spotted with the creaking failures of the Third Reich. But they were laughing. I stood transfixed as they approached us, transfixed as if this were some sort of dreamlike motion picture and I was the only spectator in that little theater back home.

All was confusion now. It felt as if this were all a blurred, slow-motion show. I watched, confused, incongruous as one of them knocked one of the girls to the floor, falling on her with fists flailing. I remember hearing little, weak cries as they moved into us. All at once I was spun around. Something struck the side of my head, and everything went black.

I don't know how long they beat us or how long afterward they left us lying in that cold, eerie room. It had all begun so quickly, in such rapid, slow-motion horror. Yet, except for those first few moments, I had mercifully been taken somewhere else.

But slowly, ever so slowly, consciousness returned. What had spun slowly in my fear and despair for Stella now turned rapidly into pain. I was in an agonizing whirlpool, and my insides churned to wretch out of me what little was in my stomach. My eyes opened, and the whirlpool began to be replaced by awareness of pain. My whole body ached and stung, as if I had been squeezed through some hole of torture too small for myself. I wondered numbly if every bone had not been broken, if I were already dead, if my body would be thrown now on the heaps of bodies I sometimes saw when they took us to work.

But that beautiful, dark-haired girl brought me back to reality. She made me realize I would once again survive. She was the first vision I recognized, lying there on the floor in my vomit.

Those beautiful green eyes stared back at me from less than a foot away. They were open wide, but frozen in horror. They were the centerpiece of an expression that spoke of unspeakable terror, a face in a perpetual grimace of death.

I stared back at that face for what must have been an hour or perhaps was but a moment that seemed to last forever. Eventually, I began to hear moans and crying about me. At least I had not been the only one to survive this beating. It meant that we had not been part of some brutal selection. It meant that we were not intended to die—at least not today. That some of us had, like the girl before my eyes, was merely an accident of chance. Still, I shivered a little as I stared into that face. I could smell his smell. I could feel the cold presence of the God of Chance. His scythe had come so close that the rush of air about it had washed over me.

As a young girl, I dreamed of love as all young girls do. Though I was too innocent to understand the realities of relationships between men and women, I, nonetheless, knew intuitively why they existed and how love played such an important role in their success or failure. My King Solomon would protect and hold me close to him. He would be gentle with me, and I would give of myself within a warm embrace of understanding, need, and mutual respect. I would be irrevocably drawn to him, whoever my King Solomon was to be. He would take his need and pleasure with me, and I would revel in sharing both intimacy and creation with him. I had dreamed of that as all young girls do. I had dreamed of giving the gift of physical and emotional love within a realm of love returned.

But my dreams lay shattered there with me on the floor of that room. As my senses slowly came back to me, I realized they had taken the last part of me I could call my own. With the callous indifference with which they so often murdered and mutilated us, they had raped me. My first experience with the physical aspects of "love" had been at the hands of the beast. But I felt nothing save the pain. I knew not my lover save the agony in my groin from his presence. I knew only a gaping new emptiness in my existence, a removal of a gift I had saved and would now never be able to replace.

The doors swung open, bathing our devastation in a swath of bright light. "Schnell! Schnell! Get up! All of you get up! Schnell!"

Wobbling, I managed to get to my feet. They rushed us out of that room as they seemed to rush us everywhere. It was as if absolutely nothing out of the ordinary had happened there. Rapidly assembling us in a naked line, they marched us out into the snow and toward a nearby building. I managed to look back into the room as we were pushed and shoved out of it. She lay there in a moment of horrible, frozen abuse, along with two other girls who didn't move when told to rise.

I remembered the building. It was the same one where Stella and I had found the little baby among the clothing of the dead. I realized they were going to give us clothes to wear. At least they intended to keep us alive for now. But I didn't feel alive. I didn't feel anything but emptiness.

The great pile of clothes once again stood before me. Had this all been but a bad nightmare? Had all the moments only been the Devil invading my subconscious? Was Mother about to roust me from my fitful sleep? Or was the dream to repeat itself? I rummaged through clothes atop the pile, for I dared not reach into it. I put on another little dress, far too light for December's cold, and managed a small jacket over it. There were no shoes, but I found a pair of sandals, little more than worn blocks of wood with leather straps over the top.

I stood there staring dumbly at the clothes after I had finished dressing. I wondered if they were going to take us back to Birkenau, back to Barrack 7. How badly I wanted to go back! Had Stella joined the green-eyed girl on some meaningless stack of bodies? Was she staring off into that cold January sky, a stark moment of lonely horror her last expression? Fear washed over me suddenly. I realized almost painfully that hope once again had taken hold of me. Would I be strong enough to hold on to it? Would I be able to survive its sapping draw on my energies? With all I had experienced the last 24 hours, I felt as if I should just throw hope atop that heap of clothing and drop dead where I stood. I was sure it was the end for me. But Stella might still be in the infirmary. She might still be breathing, and if she was, there might still be a chance I could keep my promise and somehow keep my life. I took a deep, painful breath and turned around. Without words, a kapo pointed me toward an area near the door where a few other girls now stood.

But my hopes for Stella were to remain unfulfilled. Within an hour, I found myself amid the straw of a cattle car. It was bitterly cold, but it still reeked of excrement and death. I hardly noticed, for we were little more than dead ourselves. Two men in dirty striped prisoners uniforms struggled to close the door on us. As it squealed in freezing complaint at their efforts, one of them looked in at us, and looked at none of us. Without an expression, he spoke just loudly enough not to be heard by the guards standing a few feet behind him.

"Dachau. Be careful."

The door shut out the light, and the sound of the latch locked out my hope of knowing whether Stella was still alive. But perhaps that was for the best. If I had been able to return to Barrack 7 and the infirmary, I should surely have found Mengele's truck just outside. I should surely have heard her muffled scream of death. I should surely have seen her body that night, thrown on the bunk across from me, just to make me go mad. But without knowing her fortune, there was some small bit of hope. Though I knew with near certainty they would or perhaps already had killed her, I knew with absolute certainty that she would have been dead already had I not taken her to the infirmary. How strangely the God of Chance manipulated hope! I clung now to a most uncertain hope that Stella was somehow alive. That I didn't know was a blessing of sorts. Diminished this way, hope still sustained me, but took less of my strength to maintain.

The boxcar was loaded with the sad, quiet, guttural lamentations of more separations and more moans from those who were sick. It was a cacophony of human misery and suffering in the dark confines of the car that cold day in December. I sat in the corner trying to pull further into myself, to leave life. I did not want to die, but I did not want this to be life. I listened to the cold steel sounds of the train. Over and over the wheels sang in quiet rhythm, "You left her. You left her. You left her." I felt myself dying inside, and I felt care fading away. But that glimmer of hope remained.

I didn't know it at the time, but Auschwitz and Birkenau were soon to be overrun by the Russians. Apparently, the Nazi bureaucracy thought there was still some value in the labor to be gained from thousands of emaciated prisoners. Or perhaps they thought the world would shudder even more if the Russians were to find more than a handful of living prisoners in Birkenau. The reason didn't matter, and wouldn't have mattered to any of us had we known. They had begun relocating Auschwitz-Birkenau "residents" to other camps farther away from the front. Uncle Rahamin and my brother Asher had been sent to Buchenwald. Uncle Schumuel and Joseph had gone to Mathausen (Austria) and would eventually be relocated again to Ebensee (Austria). The God of Chance dictated my relocation to Dachau.

We arrived in the camp late that evening. With the front advancing toward Auschwitz, the German's usual ordered, disciplined way of doing things had slowly begun to fall apart. There was little order to our departure from the train and much confusion as a result of our suffering. There was a damp, sinister smell to this place, not unlike the basement room of horrors in Auschwitz. But here the smell was everywhere. In Birkenau, we could smell the death from the crematories, and the bodies of the girls who electrocuted themselves each night on the wires. But here, the smell was different. Like a strange odor from wet, rotting flesh, Dachau seemed to speak to me of macabre ways to die. As if I had not already seen death in all the forms I could imagine, this place seemed as if death had been its resident keeper for a very, very long time. It made me afraid again.

The barracks here were different from those at Birkenau. They were like half-buried bunkers, with little more than their roofs showing above ground. The whole place was cold and muddy and, most of all, seemed permeated with old, unnatural death.

Our trainload of misery now entered the Dachau barracks, and after a time, I found I was with several other women from Rhodes. I hadn't seen any of them since getting on the train in Haidary, but there were no happy reunions here. There was no talk of gratitude that someone I knew had survived the beasts of Birkenau. Especially, there were no thanks given to God. By now, we hated the thought of God. We knew He either didn't exist or had given over control of our existence to chance.

I particularly had few greetings for Violet, Clara, and some of the others I had known in Rhodes. My thoughts were filled with Stella and the guilt and grief of leaving her. It didn't matter that I had no choice. It didn't matter that I had been brutalized and ripped away from her and my occasional brief conversations with the men across the fence. What mattered was that I should have been able to change something, to change somehow those events that led to Stella's internment in the infirmary and my being taken away from her, against my promise. Though no rational person would have believed I could have done anything to alter that course of events, rational thought had long since escaped me. I could not determine whether I was still a human being or simply an insane representation of one, and it mattered little. The whole world was insane.

My first morning in Dachau I was taken to clean the latrines. They were in another semiburied barrack, separate from ours, a barrack full of holes in the ground. I should have been ashamed and embarrassed to be made to do such work, but I had no pride left. The place was alive with disease, and I could feel it. I cleaned vomit and feces, urine and all manner of excrement from the floors. I wiped the inside of sinks and latrines. I washed the walls of the physical remnants of human suffering. It was inhuman to do such work in such a miserable place, but I was barely human. Most of the other girls were made to work in the German barracks where it was warm and they sometimes got a scrap or two of food. But I always worked in the latrines. Perhaps they knew my plight. Perhaps they knew I was insane and couldn't be trusted. It made no difference. I was nothing more than a robot, fast becoming the walking skeleton we all referred to as *musselman.*

Meals in Dachau were much the same as those in Birkenau. In the morning we were given the dirty, brackish water they called coffee, together with a small piece of hard, very dry dark bread. If we were lucky, we might get a bit of moldy cheese along with the bread. Our lunch was the usual soup of turnips I so hated, but I still hoped for a bit of turnip in my cup. And after a day in the latrines, I was greeted with a supper of the same hard bread we had at breakfast, together with a bit of salami or cheese.

But other than the food, things in Dachau were much different than Birkenau. There were fewer and fewer guards these days, and even the kapos seemed to be merging back into the camp populace. Though the men and women were still separated by electrified wire, the fences were not as high here. We were allowed a little more freedom to wander from barrack to barrack in Dachau, and as I walked about the camp, I always looked for a familiar face.

But I would not have recognized my father or my uncle or anyone else I knew unless they had spoken directly to me. Everyone was a walking skeleton, some barely clothed against the cold. The images I gazed upon in my wanderings were so surreal because reality itself had changed. People were not acting as people. We were all simply reacting as animals, surviving only because it was what nature brought to us through instinct. I rarely spoke, and I think for a time I forgot how. My days were filled now with excrement and the slimy life of the latrines. My nights were consumed with horrible images of my sister.

I remember wondering if one was aware one was going mad. Was there some feeling, some cognitive sense, that told you behavior was strangely odd? Was there an awareness that all was not right with that person you talk to inside yourself? I was trudging back to the barrack after spending the afternoon cleaning the latrines. I watched my feet, each step creating a sucking imprint in the mud. It was as if they were someone else's feet. It was as if I was watching another strange movie.

"Laura."

I turned briefly to look at my trail. A cold, soggy line of footprints led back to me, only the latest imprints in a field of a million others.

"Laura?"

There were little patches of wet snow here and there. I wondered numbly if those of us who threw ourselves against the electric fences each night did the kinds of things I was doing now beforehand.

"Laura!"

I turned, irritated. I knew my mind was calling my name. I knew this was madness coming over me. I was discovering there was an awareness as the mind simply let go of reality.

But there stood my old friends from Rhodes, Jaco and Salvo. They were little more than walking skeletons. My muddy trail had led me directly past them, within just a few feet, and I hadn't noticed. But I stood my ground. This could, after all, be just my crazed mind playing tricks on me.

Still, they seemed to be real. Despite their appearance, there was still that odd contrast between the two of them that no amount of abuse could erase. Jaco, tall and blonde. Salvo, much shorter and dark. I think they may have been just as disbelieving at the sight of me as I was at the sight of them. They both seemed to be transfixed, staring at me through the wires that separated us.

Jaco smiled. Though his teeth were brown from months of neglect, I could still make out that familiar grin from Rhodes that I had almost forgotten. A tiny flicker of hope ignited inside me, like the smallest match being lit in the midst of a downpour. I had assumed they were dead, like my father, my mother, and so many others. Yet here they stood before me, much the worse for wear, but apparently alive. I knew intuitively that they harbored the same kinds of thoughts.

"Do you know if my brothers are alive?"

Jaco shrugged. "They are in different camps. I don't know."

"And Uncle Rahamin? Uncle Shumuel?"

"The same. They were taken out of Birkenau the same time we were. I think Rahamin is in Mathausen. They were all alive when we left Birkenau." Jaco pursed his lips. "But now? Who knows?"

Salvo asked if I had seen his sister Sara. I told him I did not know her whereabouts. I had not seen her since well before we left Birkenau.

"Have you seen Clara?" It was Jaco, asking after his sister.

I nodded. "She is here in Dachau. She is alive. If I see her, I'll tell her you are both here. I'll tell her to try and meet with you here."

Jaco shook his head. "No, Laura. Don't. I know she's alive. That is enough." He approached the fence, and motioned for me to do the same. "Salvo and I are going to escape. We have arranged it with two of the Polish men. Do you want to join us?"

I stared at the two of them. They looked so full of despair and hopelessness, as I'm sure I did to them. Jaco had a long stubble of beard over his gaunt face. Salvo's skin was dark and blotchy, probably the result of some infection he didn't know, or didn't care, he had. But there was obviously still a degree of hope in these two. They were going to risk themselves to escape this madness that was Dachau, this insanity fostered by the Reich that had long enveloped all of us. I nodded. I said yes.

How far from reality were we all that we could even imagine escape? Where would we escape to, here in the middle of Germany? How could we possibly imagine that survival in this world of war would be any easier than it was here in Dachau, given our circumstances? This was insanity. It had to be. Surely, I should simply throw myself at the wires. But that little flicker of flame that the sight of Jaco and Salvo had ignited within me still glowed. Any existence, any chance of existence with hope, was better than this existence with none. Salvo told me to meet them at this same place after dark.

I don't remember walking back to the barrack or anything else of that afternoon. I don't even remember if I told Clara that Jaco was alive. It didn't matter. Jaco had said nothing of asking Clara to join the escape. Obviously, there was much danger in this. Would it have been better for Clara to know? Would it have been better for her to wonder about her brother, to worry about his survival on top of her own struggle to exist? To this day, I don't know whether I had the inner strength to deal with the question or not, and I don't remember if circumstances that day would have permitted a whispered conversation with Jaco's sister.

I found myself back at the spot that evening. It was snowing a little, and I peered through the dim light of the camp for what seemed like hours. There was such quiet madness to this. The snow swirled about my small field of vision as so many thousand odd thoughts wandered through my mind. I realized I was shivering, and I welcomed it, for it was not from the wet cold that permeated existence here in Dachau. I was afraid. It meant I actually felt something, and I realized it! My mind embraced my fear, clung to it like the sight of a lighthouse in a storm of insanity. I wondered how I managed to care if I should live through this or die trying. I peered through the snow for a sign of them.

"Laura!"

I could barely hear it. An almost whispered name wandering to my ears through the snowflakes.

"Laura, go back."

I discerned the direction of the call and realized it came from the back of a truck parked a distance away from the wires.

"Laura, go back. Go back to the barrack." I couldn't tell whether the voice was Jaco's or Salvo's, but the language was Ladino. Something had gone wrong. Someone had noticed.

"We are sorry, Laura. Go back. Good-bye, Laura. Good-bye!"

Instinctively, I turned away from the direction of the voice. I tried to immerse myself in a dark area a little way from where I had waited, but where I could still see the truck without being noticed myself.

There were no guards apparent to me, but it was obvious they had been caught. I stood in shock there in the darkness, not wanting to accept what was happening before my eyes.

"Good-bye!"

I heard the sound of the truck starting, of doors slamming shut. I felt the flicker of hope within me go out with little more than the hiss of the Devil. I watched the back of the truck begin to move and fade into the darkness.

I don't remember how long I stood there in that cold, muddy blackness. I just listened to the sound of the snow as it covered the day's footprints. In perhaps a moment, in perhaps an hour, Jaco and Salvo would be dead, shot efficiently and left in a snowbank somewhere outside the camp. I wondered dully if I would hear the shots before I finished the short walk back to the barrack.

I took a deep, halting breath as the lighthouse went dark. At least, I thought, we got to say good-bye.

I shivered again, but only from the cold. The snow, falling harder now, seemed to mute the sound of my footsteps as I trudged back to hopelessness.

It had been a while since I'd had to bury another atrocity. With the advancing Russian front, much of the Germans' resources had been devoted to what they felt were more important things than murder and butchery. But to believe that life for us prisoners was easier was to believe in the absurd. We had, these days, even less to eat than before the war had begun to go bad for our captors. We still lived in absolute filth, cold, and misery. We still existed in a world without hope. There were simply fewer Nazis around these days to terrorize and humiliate. There were simply fewer new ideas of what one could do to a helpless individual. But we were still prisoners, and the Germans were still capable of the efficient slaughter we had witnessed time and again since coming to Birkenau.

They probably thought I was insane, and I probably was. While most of the other girls tended to the German barracks, I spent days on end in the stench of the latrines. I worried constantly over Stella's fate, though my promise to Mother seemed somehow less crucial these days. I also wondered what really happened to Jaco and Salvo, their incident being far fresher in my consciousness. I had heard no gunshots, so perhaps they had somehow survived. My mind hoped for them, but my heart knew better. Our murder had seldom been borne of emotion. At best, we were simply a low-value labor pool to support the German arms industry. At worst, we were only a nuisance that had long since been controlled and was fast being exterminated. Jaco and Salvo were just another execution, like so many before them, and the shots had simply been beyond hearing.

Yet, before Dachau would become another loss, the Nazis managed a new idea, a new means to rid themselves of the scourge of our belief.

Laura (age 8) and Stella (age 4) at the Purim carnival, Rhodes 1934.

(Back to front) Uncle Jaco, Laura, Reina, Shumuel, Asher, Stella, Solomon, cousin Jaco, Diana, and Joseph. Rhodes, 1937.

The Varon family with Grandma Rachel at center and Laura kneeling at bottom right, 1935.

Auntie Diana, 1938.

Auntie Fortune, 1938.

(Left to right) Laura, Joseph, Asher, Stella, and Jaco, 1939.

Uncle Nissim in Leopoldville, 1939.

Auntie Diana and Uncle Shumuel with little Jaco, 1939.

(Clockwise from left) Asher, Joseph, Stella, and Jaco, 1939.

On a picnic in Trianda. Laura is kneeling at bottom right.

Laura with Nurse Ingrid in Sweden after the war.

Laura in Sweden, 1946.

Laura and Stella, Merano, Italy, 1947.

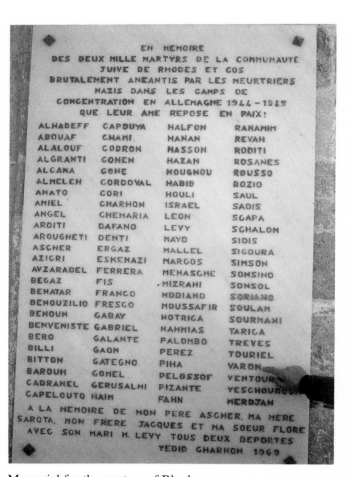

EN MEMOIRE
DES DEUX MILLE MARTYRS DE LA COMMUNAUTE
JUIVE DE RHODES ET COS
BRUTALEMENT ANEANTIS PAR LES MEURTRIERS
NAZIS DANS LES CAMPS DE
CONCENTRATION EN ALLEMAGNE 1944 - 1945
QUE LEUR AME REPOSE EN PAIX!

ALHADEFF	CAPOUYA	HALFON	RAHAMIM
ABOUAF	CHAMI	HANAN	REVAH
ALALOUF	CODRON	HASSON	RODITI
ALGRANTI	COHEN	HAZAN	ROSANES
ALCANA	GONE	HOUGNOU	ROUSSO
ALMELEH	CORDOVAL	HABIB	ROZIO
AMATO	CORI	HOULI	SAUL
AMIEL	CHARHON	ISRAEL	SADIS
ANGEL	CHEMARIA	LEON	SCAPA
AROITI	DAFANO	LEVY	SCHALOM
AROUGHETI	DENTI	MAYO	SIDIS
ASCHER	ERGAZ	MALLEL	SIGOURA
AZICRI	ESKENAZI	MARGOS	SIMSON
AVZARADEL	FERRERA	MENASCHE	SONSINO
BEGAZ	FIS	MIZRAHI	SONSOL
BENATAR	FRANCO	MODIANO	SORIANO
BENOUZILIO	FRESCO	MOUSSAFIR	SOULAM
BENOUN	GABAY	NOTRICA	SOURMANI
BENVENISTE	GABRIEL	NAHMIAS	TARICA
BERO	GALANTE	PALOMBO	TREVES
BILLI	GAON	PEREZ	TOURIEL
BITTON	GATEGNO	PIHA	VARON
BAROUH	GOMEL	PELOSSOF	VENTOURA
CADRANEL	GERUSALMI	PIZANTE	YESCHOUROU
CAPELOUTO	HAIM	FAHN	MERDJAN

A LA MEMOIRE DE MON PERE ASCHER, MA MERE
SAROTA, MON FRERE JACQUES ET MA SOEUR FLORE
AVEC SON MARI M. LEVY TOUS DEUX DEPORTES
YEDID CHARHON 1969

Memorial for the martyrs of Rhodes.

5.

DESPAIR

IN MANY WAYS, I was reminded of that day we walked down to the boats in Rhodes. We were loosely assembled in a long line, four or five abreast, that stretched as far as I could see. But in the last days of February 1945, the outskirts of Munich were in total ruin. In the cold and wet snow that surrounded our long line, the remains of bombed-out buildings and homes stood in stark, blackened contrast to the white of winter. The world had truly turned upside down. In my half-mad mind's eye, the whitewashed, sun-baked buildings of home had somehow turned to a burned, blackened shell under the gray skies.

Uncharacteristically, there had been little organization to our departure from Dachau. We had simply been gathered from all corners of the camp and assembled loosely near the gate. From there, under guard, we began walking.

I had no idea where we were being taken, and I believe that at least some of our guards had no idea either. We seemed to march endlessly, sometimes in circles that spanned many miles. Many in the line simply dropped of exhaustion. Many were shot for reasons known only to their murderers.

Most of the time, I was unaware of those around me. I simply walked, head down, watching my feet fall one in front of the other, much as I had done before I first saw Jaco and Salvo in Dachau. My thoughts, though numb, were consumed with grief and guilt over Stella and continued questioning the fates of my two friends. With the exhaustion and cold, it was all becoming simply too much. I began to rationalize that survival was a worthless exercise. If only I could stop walking. If only I could just lie down here in the road and fall asleep forever.

"Do not sit down. Keep going. Keep going." It was Yiddish, and it came from the woman beside me. Over and over she would urge me, keeping me alive. The words began to ring in my ears and, somehow, some way, my feet kept falling one in front of the other.

We stopped in many camps over many, many days. If we happened to arrive when the prisoners in a camp were being fed, then we were fed. If we happened to arrive at a different time, we went without food for yet another day.

For their part, the guards along our line seemed to enjoy telling us they were marching us to our deaths. Though most of them seemed to be showing the signs of their falling society, their machine guns still worked flawlessly, and their hatred and disdain for us was stronger than it had ever been. They would usually shoot anyone who fell, spattering the mud and snow with the crimson result of bigotry. I believe their malevolence increased during the marches because it was fueled with the fear borne of impending defeat. I believed, and still do, that the guards led many prisoners to their deaths by simply marching them in endless circles until they fell.

But our march seemed to have purpose. We seemed to be going somewhere, because as the days passed so, too, we passed through many camps and towns. When we would approach the outskirts of towns, the air raid sirens would be sounded to warn the townspeople to go inside and close their window blinds. In this way, the Nazis tried to hide us from their own people, tried to make them believe that none of this existed.

But even in the most terrible society ever to rise, there was humanity. I remember one town where, from the corner of my eye, I saw the flutter of a window blind from a gray building. And when I looked down, an apple lay on the ground at my feet. It seemed so impossible, so improbable that I and others near me stopped, an action we could easily have been shot for. Yet we were so surprised by that small act of kindness that we could not move. Another person had acted as a human being in this sea of inhumanity. Someone had thrown an apple. Someone had reached out into our chasm of suffering with an act of kindness, freely given. I thought I had long since forgotten how to cry. I thought I had long ago shut away as much emotion as I could survive without. But I felt a tear, a genuine tear, wandering down my cheek.

"Why does she cry?"

In an instant, I froze into the humble stance I had learned to take in front of Germans. It was one of the guards, one of our tormentors, and he was talking to the woman next to me about *me*.

"She is cold."

I shuddered, but managed to maintain my composure, such as it was.

"Where is she from? Some sunny place?"

"She is from Rhodes. The island of Rhodes."

The guards eyes grew large. He was an older man, probably in his fifties, who had obviously been conscripted or "volunteered" to serve once again for his country. He was not SS, but Vermacht.

"Just a minute. Just a minute." He fumbled in an inside pocket of his uniform. I was virtually certain he was about to pull out a gun and shoot me.

The guard now faced me directly, excited. He held a picture from his wallet before my eyes.

"Do you know him? Have you seen him? He is my son. Did you ever see him in Rhodes?"

He stood before me like a child looking for candy. For a moment, just a moment in time, we were two people again. He was a father, asking me, as a person, if I knew of his son. At another time and in another place, I would have done him a kindness and told him I had seen his son. But I was not myself, I was only a walking little bit of nothing. I could not answer. I could not think. I could not help a German, any German, after all that had been done to us.

But I did remember the young man in the picture. That look of profound sadness, of profound regret, was in the picture just as it had been on Rhodes. He was the young German soldier I had passed near Izguro. The one who said nothing, but only looked at me with those sad, sad eyes. They were eyes that had seen more than a young person should see. I wonder today if at times I have the same expression.

I shook my head.

"She has not seen him," the woman next to me said.

"Not ever?"

I trembled again. "Never."

The days of marching seemed to run into one another, seemed to become a constant, gray carpet of sadness, punctured here and there with the scars of war. It was bitterly cold, and many died at night, leaning up against the wall of a barn or some other place we were sequestered. I stumbled and stepped over bodies in the road, some still warm after simply falling of exhaustion, some beaten to death, some shot. We stopped to work in many camps and industrial areas, to scrape and clean scrap metal for more ammunition the Germans now didn't have time to manufacture.

Somewhere near the Austrian Alps, I found myself sitting cross-legged in a group of women, scraping metal beside a huge pile of scrap, We were inside a bombed-out industrial building, its girders supporting nothing now but the gray sky. We had been here for two days and had had no food for three days.

"Come. Come with me."

I continued scraping metal, only half aware that the words had been directed at me.

"You. You from Rhodes. Come with me. Come with me."

I turned at hearing the name of Rhodes. The old Vermacht guard stood near me, looking straight at me.

"Come. Come. Don't be afraid."

But I was terrified. Was he about to shoot me because I had not said I had seen his son? Would he take me into the snow outside and beat me to death? But I had no choice. If I refused, I knew I would die. At least to follow him meant I would live a few moments longer.

He led me to a small shack just outside the remains of the factory. There was a small chimney, and wisps of smoke blew away from it in the wind. He opened the door, and motioned for me to enter ahead of him. Surely, he was about to rape me and leave me to die. Certainly, I was to be shot.

A large pot sat atop a cast iron stove, and I could hear it boiling whatever liquid it contained. The old soldier ladled a cup of the liquid, placing it on a small table between us.

"Here. Sit and eat. Don't be afraid."

I didn't move from where I stood near the door. Though the inside of the shack was warm, I shivered in fear. I was frozen to the spot where I stood, and he could see my obvious terror.

He looked at me with a look I shall never forget. A strange look of compassion in this world of terror. A look I had never expected to see again. A look I would never have expected from a German. He almost smiled and at first, simply motioned for me to sit down.

But I just stood there. A strange combination of disbelief and stark fear held me in a grip so tight I could barely breathe.

He shrugged and walked past me to the door. "Please. Sit here and eat. Don't be afraid. You must eat."

And with that, he left me alone in the shack. He shut the door behind him.

I did not understand then, and I do not understand today, why this man showed kindness to me. I will never understand why he singled me out for that moment of humanness in so many months of brutality. Perhaps he knew I was lying and hoped I would tell him of his son. Surely he wanted something in exchange for this risk. Surely he expected a return for his investment of kindness.

It was easy to confuse anyone who was as near to death as we were. We were so undernourished, so cold and miserable, that the mind no longer functioned with any degree of reliable, conscious thought. I stood there, confounded at this kindness from the old man. I stood there, knowing from experience that I could not trust any German.

Yet I had to trust him. I had no choice. If I left the shack, particularly without the escort of a guard, I would be shot. If I stayed, I might be shot anyway. As confused and frightened as I was, my inclination was to do nothing. As hungry as I was, I sat at the table and, haltingly, ate the soup he had ladled for me.

I don't remember if I ever was warmed by the little shack's stove. I don't remember what the soup tasted like, though I do recall it contained pasta, something I had only dreamed of tasting again. My only memory after that moment is finding myself again sitting crosslegged, scraping metal and saying nothing, worrying about Stella and Jaco and Salvo, and wondering why the old soldier had risked his life for the sake of my full stomach.

The march seemed to go on forever. From the soggy, snowy fields of southern Germany, we had wound our way through the foothills of the Austrian Alps and were now wandering through the northern forests. There were so many trees, dark and oppressive in their size and silence. They were like quiet witnesses to our plight, quiet watchers of the long line of despondent humanity beneath them. How many died in that whispering cold I can only imagine. How many secrets the forests hold are known only to God.

But we trudged on, and on, and on. Somewhere in those high hills of forest, I remember suddenly feeling the sun on my shoulders. It

was so cold, I had long since stopped shivering. I had long since
forgotten the warmth of that little shack. I had long since forgotten
sensation itself. Yet the light somehow stirred my awareness. I looked
up and found myself staring at a sign framed in the glare of the sun.

Ebensee. Another camp in hundreds of camps. Another place of
death. Another place of brutal forced labor. We didn't stop. We didn't
eat at this place, but for some reason, I would remember the name.

Of all the towns and camps and places we passed on the march,
Ebensee is the only name I recall. Was it the rare sunshine that made
the name stay in my mind? Was it the cold or some other strange
coincidence that forced the letters into my numbed memory?

In the Holocaust I was a part of, I learned how unbelievably brutal
one human being can be to another. I learned of despair and the
truest meanings of hopelessness. I understood what it meant to have
your sense of home destroyed, and how the smallest acts of kindness,
regardless of their motivation, can mean more than anything else to
the human spirit. And I learned that God still lived. Whatever impossible, implausible reasons He had for allowing His people to be
so decimated and abused, I learned that He still cared. While I remained angry and embittered that my God could have permitted it
to happen, I have come to understand that He did not forget us. I
have come to understand, as is shown in Ecclesiastes, that God was
not to blame:

"Consider God's doing! Who can straighten what He has twisted?
So in a time of good fortune enjoy the good fortune: and in a time
of misfortune, reflect: The one no less than the other was God's
doing; consequently, man may find no fault with him."

Years later I would learn that both my brothers and Uncle Shumuel
were in Ebensee when that long, horrible march passed through. The
moment I saw that sign against the sky may well have been the
moment of Uncle Shumuel's death. The God of Chance, after all,
was everywhere around us.

There had been many days during that march when I knew I could
not go on. There was so much death. There was so much brutality,
bolstered as it was by the fear of our keepers. Though we often heard
the bombs fall along the way, and sometimes the rumble of artillery,
there was nothing to hope for. Whether on the first day of our incarceration or the last, we existed in a different world. It was a realm
where even our sense of time became muddied, and where truth

could not be discerned from rumor. As such, I had learned long ago to view any small bits of information regarding the progress of the war as likely concoctions of those of us grasping for the last few straws of hope. I believed nothing unless it was proven before my eyes. Those who would one day find us, who would shudder and vomit at the sight of heaped bodies, would say they didn't believe the rumors of the camps they'd heard during the war. They'd say in tears they didn't believe such rumors—until the unique smell of rotting flesh slapped them to their senses.

I suppose we were like them in that respect, but for far different reasons. They had hope. Hope of restored peace. Hope of victory. Hope of family and all that is good. They had hope, and stumbling into the camps, they found the evidence of utter hopelessness. We, on the other hand, were the still-living part of that devastation. We would not, and could not, believe there was hope until, in tears, it would stand before us.

What had been a line that seemed to stretch to the horizon when we left Dachau now shuffled along in small disorganized groups. We were emaciated when we had begun this journey to nowhere. We were decimated, walking corpses as we stumbled the last few hundred yards into Bergen-Belsen. No one knew that this was our destination. For the most part, we just thought this was yet another camp among the many we had stopped in. Perhaps there would be food here.

But I soon realized that this place was the last stop on our long journey through Germany. There was food here, though precious little of it. There was also dysentery, typhus, and a host of other maladies that the God of Chance sprinkled among us. And unlike Birkenau and, to a lesser extent, Dachau, there was little discipline in Bergen-Belsen. Certainly, we were bullied about and brutalized just as we had always been, but there was no regimen, no routine to the ways of our captors. As the days passed, we realized there was no work to do in Bergen-Belsen, save moving those who died each night from inside our barrack to the rows of bodies piled in the space between the barracks. And there were no selections here. It was as if the Nazis had organized this place as a final collection point for those of us who had somehow survived. With rare exception, their collection consisted of thousands of walking skeletons, of Polish and Russian and Ukranian and Czechoslovakian musselmen. There were

no selections here because this *was* the final selection. There was no
need to expend the bullets. Disease and starvation would take care
of what was left of us. Within this living grave, we had more freedom
of movement than in any of the other camps. Perhaps it was an
expression of perverted sympathy on the part of the Nazis. We could
at least choose the spot inside the fences where we could take our
last breath.

How strange, then, that I should find a companion here. At first,
we had not recognized each other but from the sound of our speech.
Laurina and I stumbled across each other as we both happened to
seek the same water spigot at the same time. Laurina, who had
watched Rhodes fall away into the darkness with me; Laurina, who
had taken my same journey; who had somehow survived selections
in Birkenau; who had walked with me at times in the mud of Dachau.
We had been in the same long line that had withered as we wandered
through the Reich. But I had not seen her. Until the proof stood as
an odd-looking set of bones before me, I had assumed she and all
the rest of Rhodes were dead.

We both wept but could shed no tears. She held me for a moment,
and I her.

"At least we can die together here."

But Laurina had an inner strength that I had long since lost. "We
will survive, Laura," she said. "We must survive. There are rumors
the Allies will be here soon. We must hold on to that, Laura. We
must live."

From that moment on, we were together constantly. Laurina and
I slept side by side in the stench of the barrack. Every morning, we
carried the bodies of our sisters who died during the night to the
ever-growing piles. As I lost strength from diarrhea, Laurina would
prop me up against her and pick the lice from my hair. And as the
seldom-given meals dwindled to nothing, as I now no longer had
strength to walk, Laurina would bring me water. After a time, we
stopped carrying the bodies outside. We simply dragged them to the
center of the room, creating an ever-growing pile among those of us
who still breathed.

There was nothing else for us, save our struggle to save each other.
I had no strength to give her, no words of encouragement for her
moments of need. But I believe I saved Laurina just as surely as she
saved me. I existed, and I was alive, though barely. The effort to

keep me among the living was Laurina's reason for living. She was my friend, my companion, my sister, my mother. I was her reason.

"I think maybe we should make a pact, Laura."

I looked up at her from where I lay on the floor. She was sitting against the barrack wall beside me, staring numbly at the pile of bodies in the middle of the room.

"A pact?" I whispered.

She nodded almost imperceptibly. "You know, a last will. If I die, you find my family and tell them of this. You tell them everything." She looked down at me to see that I was paying attention. She continued as she looked back at the bodies. "And if you die, Laura, I promise I will do the same."

I reached over to touch her forearm. I didn't ask what would become of the pact if all our families were dead. I didn't ask because I was beginning to believe we would both be dead soon, so it wouldn't matter anyway.

"I promise, Laurina, I promise." She continued to stare at the bodies, but touched my hand as if to seal our agreement.

But things had become worse. Most of us, Laurina included, now had no strength to remove the bodies. We slept among the dead and spent our days staring at them. We spoke only when there was compelling reason to. And more and more just fell asleep forever. We didn't know why the Nazis closed and locked the doors to the barrack, and most of us didn't care any more. There were more dead in the building than there were living, and those of us who still opened our eyes had begun to believe that death was a welcome escape.

Still, Laurina maintained a degree of hope, though perhaps she maintained the facade for me. I remember closing my eyes. I remember how the pains associated with my hunger and sickness suddenly left me. I remember the glimmer of a light from the darkness of my subconscious.

"Laura! Wake up, Laura! There are uniforms outside. Strange uniforms!" She shook me as she peered through the barrack window.

"Laura! Wake up."

"Leave me alone. Let me sleep. Let me die." I closed my eyes again and felt the pain begin to quickly fall away. I began to feel myself drifting inexorably away from myself, and I began to see that odd light again.

But something was wrong. The light came from the frame of the barrack doors, and there were huge men standing in the middle of it. I blinked and realized I was conscious. I blinked again and saw the rays of light streaming from where the soldiers stood. And despite the brightest rays of warm sunlight I have ever seen, I saw their faces.

I saw their tears of disbelief. I saw their tears of shame. I saw their hands in a taught salute, quivering at the grisly humanity they honored.

The gypsy woman had been right about those strange uniforms and the danger they would present. But she had been so frightened by her vision that she had forgotten to tell me the end of the story. These new, strange uniforms bore hope, carried as they were on the reemergence of God from the abyss. The light around them enveloped me, and the God of Chance melted away.

I decided to stay awake. For reasons known only to Him, God had decided that Laurina and I should survive to tell the story. I weighed about 50 pounds.

6.

REDEMPTION

MOMENTS AFTER THAT TEARFUL SALUTE, the soldiers turned and closed the doors. I didn't know why they left, but I didn't care. I knew they'd be back. I knew that at last this long storm had broken.

After an hour or so the doors again opened, and that blinding light covered us all. But this time, the soldiers were replaced by men in strange-looking yellow suits. They began spraying a white, talcum-like powder over us, over the dead, over everything. It was DDT to kill the billions of lice, ticks, and fleas that had been sucking what little life was left in us for months.

And almost before I knew what was happening, I was in the arms of my liberator. He carried me, like a limp, light little doll, from where I had prepared to die to the back of a truck just outside the barrack. In that moment, a little less than nine months since we had stepped aboard the ships in Rhodes, I finally lost my fear.

The back of the truck was open, and together with the few others they had placed there, I watched in amazement at what was transpiring just outside the barrack. There were what seemed like hundreds of soldiers, all moving about with maddening speed. They were like crazed beings, going from place to place, trying to do so many things at one time. It seemed as if they didn't know where to start. Should they tend to the living? Remove, perhaps, the taught-skinned skeletons of the dead? How could this horrible, unspeakable excrement of the Nazis be erased? As all good armies do, they knew only one course of action, to attack. But the assault was futile. The dead were dead. The dying would still die, no matter what they tried to do. And a few of us, by chance and the help of God, would live.

Perhaps it was that I had been accustomed to watching the slow onslaught of death. Perhaps all those men, healthy and full of life, weren't really moving as quickly as my weak vision perceived. It didn't matter. What I perceived at that moment was as important as any sight I have ever set my eyes on. The sense of urgency, the rapidity of movement, the constant motion of those men in uniform, was magically infectious to those of us near death. To this day, I believe it was just enough to affirm my decision of an hour before not to give up.

It was time to live again. I didn't stop to think if I was making the right choice. I didn't stop, lying there in the back of that truck, to consider whether or not I had anything to live for. I didn't pause to reflect that there might not be a single member of my family left alive, save me. But fear had left me. The freedom of that alone was enough to live for.

Ever so gently, they lifted a few more of us into the back of the truck. Moments later, a soldier carefully lifted the gate, ever so quietly latching it in place. He looked up for a second, and his eyes caught mine.

"Hello. I love you."

The soldier smiled at me sadly. The only other English words I knew were "good-bye."

I found myself lying in a little bed in the middle of a huge room full of little beds, and full of women like me. It was noisy compared to the quiet whispers of the barrack, but I welcomed the sounds of life, especially the carefully given food. Here and there, doctors and nurses busily tended to us, and light, wonderful and warm, streamed through the windows. At some point after the truck had arrived, they had cleaned me, shaved my hair, and dressed me in a white linen hospital gown. I lay there quietly now, watching and looking and reveling in the absence of fear and the stench of death. The sheets on the bed were cool and soft and so very, very white. It was almost too much to believe. I drifted off to an uncertain sleep, unsure if this was reality or merely the last bitter trick of death.

I felt a touch on my shoulder. It was almost as gentle as the feel of the sheets that covered me. Slowly, that touch brought me out of that troubled sleep, and a full day of intermittent, confusing dreams. A tall, beautiful woman stood next to my bed. Her eyes were set wide apart above high cheekbones. Her hair, elegantly styled, sat high on her head. She had that self-assured demeanor that could inspire confidence in those around her: Confidence that she would take care of them; confidence that she would take care of me. She spoke flawless Italian. A calm, reassuring voice that was full of compassion and certainty.

"What is your name, little one?"

My voice came in little more than a hoarse whisper. "Laura. Laura Varon."

"And where did you come from, before the camps, Laura?" Her eyes moved between mine and the clipboard she was writing on.

"I am from *Rhodos*. The Isle of Rhodes."

"Mmmm. I see." She continued writing on the clipboard as I watched her. After a moment she pulled a stool next to the bed, sat down, and leaned forward toward me, as if she were about to tell me a secret. Her voice became as soft as her touch.

"Laura. You are a very sick girl. You have both dysentery and typhus from the lice. You are going to need a long time to get better, and special care, too."

The news of the exact nature of my sickness neither startled nor worried me. I knew I was very sick. I had almost let myself die. The cause was of little consequence.

"We want to take you to Sweden to get better. Tomorrow we will put you on a truck to Hamburg, and from there you will go on to Sweden for your recuperation."

I began to weep. Dry, desperate little tears that barely fell from my eyes before drying.

"I, I don't want to go to Sweden. I can't go to Sweden!"

The woman again touched my shoulder. "Why, Laura?"

"I promised my mother in Auschwitz that we would meet after the war in Italy. I have to go to Italy! They will think I am dead if I don't go to Italy."

"Where in Italy, Laura?"

"*Milano*. Milan. I have to go to Milan."

She smiled a pursed-lip smile, and her eyes left mine. "I'll see what we can do for you, Laura. I'll see. But you know, Laura, even if we have to take you to Sweden, the Red Cross will let your family know where you are, and why."

"*Milano*," I repeated.

"We'll see."

In retrospect, I will never be able to say enough about that tall, elegant woman or the doctors and nurses who tended to us so carefully. It was far more than the quality of their care for which I love them all so much. It was the fact that they were considerate, respectful, civilized human beings who understood our condition both physically and emotionally. That tall woman never once mentioned that my relatives might all be dead. She didn't try to force me to go to Sweden the instant she had broached the subject. She and the others who cared for us were, first and foremost, considerate of the torment and anguish we all carried within us. They made the shock of our introduction back into the civilized world as gentle a transition as was humanely possible. And shock though it still was, its edges were softened by those doctors, nurses, and the serene, wonderful woman with the gentle touch. I only wish I remembered her name.

The next morning, of course, that same tall woman came back and told me I was simply too ill to travel to Italy. She assured me again that the Red Cross would inform my relatives of my whereabouts. She never once said anything about the fact that there might well be no relatives left to inform. Reluctantly, I agreed to go to Sweden. Though it was never put to me as an "order," I knew inside that I really had no choice in the matter. There was no point in arguing with the woman. I barely had strength to whisper.

Within hours, Laurina and I were again in the back of a truck headed for Hamburg. Late that afternoon, they put us on a small ship destined for Sweden.

One by one, they carried us from the trucks to the ship. Even those who could walk, like Laurina, were carried across the gangplank, into the cabin, and placed on lounge chairs, most of which were near windows. It took more than an hour for all of us to board the ship. Laurina and I huddled in chairs next to each other, covered with blankets to stay warm. By the time the ship got underway, Laurina was fast asleep, and I was left alone with the approaching dusk, alone with my thoughts.

I became uneasy as dusk turned to darkness. There were too many reminders here of how this had all begun. Once again, I was on a ship heading into the darkness of uncertainty. Once again, I could feel the too-familiar thump of the ship's propeller. The darkness enveloped me, surrounded me in loneliness. I wondered if Stella had somehow survived. I thought about Joseph and Asher, hoping against hope that they had somehow escaped the gas. And for the first time in many months, I allowed myself to think of Father and Mother. I could still see Mother's face in my mind's eye. I could still hear her voice: "Take care of Stella. Meet us in Italy." I could still see Father's tear-stained face through the wire. But I didn't cry for them as I thought I would. I drew a deep, halting breath and peered out into the darkness. I had never felt so alone.

I don't remember if I slept those two days aboard ship. I don't remember if I ate or drank or talked with Laurina. It seemed as if I just stared out that window, watching the gray skies and the whitecaps of the North Sea. It was, after all, but a few days since I had been embroiled in the nightmare. It was but tens of hours since I had slept with the dead, since I had almost decided to join them. It was the first time I had been without the inner turmoil of fear, the first time I had been alone and unthreatened. Fear had left me, yes, but now I had to deal with the demons of its passing. As weak as I was, I imagined that, if I let certain memories creep back to my consciousness, I should surely die.

I tried to concentrate on life. I tried to keep all those horrible memories in my subconscious where I had thrust them the moment they occurred. But it was not easy. If I closed my eyes, I could see that baby in the clothes pile. If I looked too long at Laurina's face, I was reminded of the gaunt stare on the faces of the dead. If I focused more than a moment on the voices around me, I heard Jaco and Salvo as the Nazis took them away or the last whispers of the pregnant woman the Nazis butchered. It was not easy. There was little here to fill my thoughts, except wondering if my family still existed, the uncertainty of where my life might lead, and the graceful, dipping seagulls that followed the ship into the night.

When we arrived in Malmo, Sweden, they took us from the ship directly to a tent hospital that had been erected in a park along the beach. It was extremely well organized, with beds and examining areas and medical equipment of every kind. And there were what seemed to be hundreds of doctors and nurses to help us. What struck me about the place was how different it was than the hospital days earlier at Bergen-Belsen. Here, the doctors walked about with purpose; the nurses seemed to know exactly what to expect and precisely what to do with us. Here, no one was reacting to the horror of a thousand dead or the confusion of what to do with those still living. Here, the people charged with our care purposefully dealt with the physical results of our holocaust.

They shaved me again, everywhere. The DDT had killed the lice, but there were still likely to be eggs in any place on our bodies the first shaving had missed. Laurina and I were separated because her sickness was judged not to be as serious as mine, and not contagious as mine was. It frightened me. It reminded me of a selection.

But I was instantly reassured by the smiles of the doctors and the gentle touch of nurses who seemed to tend to us constantly. They took me to a hot, steam-filled room full of tubs of hot water. They helped me bathe, scrubbed my skin with coarse brushes, helped me stand in a cold shower, then repeated the process over and over again. My skin, clinging to what little muscle was left on my bones, had become a hard, greenish-yellow leather covering me. They bathed, scrubbed, and showered me many times to begin to restore circulation, to bring back some degree of normal color to my pallish countenance.

I suppose that when society remembers the Holocaust, the focus tends to be on its horrors, on the incredible abuse and inhumanity the Nazis forced on us. But I remember, too, the wisdom and rapid response to our plight from those who cared for us afterward. Those three British soldiers who stood in the door of the barrack might as well have been the entire army. By the thousands, we were dead men walking among piles of dead men, and we caused them all to stop and reflect on the horrors of bigotry. But they only stopped for a moment. I remember how those soldiers, calloused and hardened by war, ran about the camp in feverish attempts to save all who could be saved. I remember how gentle they were, yet how quickly they extracted us, pausing only long enough to retch at the sight of the bodies or the putrid smell of the dead.

Within hours of discovering Bergen-Belsen, the Swedish royal family arranged for the transport and care of those of us who were most seriously ill. From my small perspective, it was as if an entire nation had become mobilized to care for us. There was always someone there to tend to my sickness, to tell me what was happening to me, or to just listen to me cry. I had never been to Sweden; it was a very strange and cold place for me. But I will never, never forget the people who lived there, the nation of humanity that cared. I owe them my life.

In the aftermath of Bergen-Belsen, General Eisenhower walked among the bodies in rage. He ordered the German people nearby to come and see what they had allowed. He ordered them to bury the dead. And he called every general in his army to see the Nazi butchery. And he called the press. Nearly every correspondent in Europe at the time visited Bergen-Belsen, saw and smelled the death, filmed and wrote of the unspeakable. "I want the world to see and record this," Eisenhower told his aides, "because twenty or thirty years from now people will try to deny this ever happened."

Of course, I knew none of this at the time. I knew only the gentle British soldier who carried me out of the barrack. I knew only the wonderful, elegant woman in the hospital who respected me as human. I knew only the careful, gentle care I was given by the Swedish doctors and nurses. History and experience have given me the perspective that that care and concern I felt extended all the way to the highest levels of nations. And more than that, I will remember the wisdom of the Allied general. More than any other single person, he allowed the world to see the horror, allowed the world to grieve and care, allowed the world to understand the terror I lived through so that it should never happen again.

But it would be many months before I could thank anyone, many weeks before I had the strength to utter little more than hoarse whispers. From the tent hospital in Malmo, I was taken by truck to board a train headed for the city of Ystad. Those of us who were most contagious, they told us, were to be taken there and hospitalized. When we boarded the ship, they carried each of us to compartments aboard the train. I laid atop a small bed.

It's odd how quickly the mind can begin to restore itself, to deal with life rather than death. As they took us to our compartments, I was reminded again of my trip into the nightmare of the camps. But I took notice of the cleanliness of the compartment, the smooth, clean feel of the bed, and I tried to erase the thoughts of similarity between this train and another, a far more brutal one I had been on. My mind seemed now to dwell on what was good, to quell recollection of past horrors. Nonetheless, there would be many times those thoughts of what happened would spring to my consciousness. Like demons, they would jump before my eyes to terrorize me and make me doubt the evil had really ended.

I shared the compartment with a girl named Sima. She was a little older than I and managed to speak with me in broken Italian. I never knew her true nationality, but she told me she had come to Bergen-Belsen from Therienstadt. Though she seemed to be considerably healthier than I, she, too, had been judged to be contagious. At least she spoke in a near normal voice. Though I hadn't looked in a mirror, I saw in her what must have been a near mirror image of me. She was nearly a walking skeleton, and she was completely shaved and was bald. Her eyes were sunk deep in her face and appeared as if she had been hit in both of them.

Sima didn't say much as the train got underway, and I couldn't. We both seemed to avoid talk about what we had endured. We both were trying to focus, I think, on life again. We shared few words, but pleasant ones. And then, as the train passed the outskirts of Malmo, we came into the tulip fields.

Sima managed to stand up, her hands against the window. I sat up on my little bunk, and we both just stared. I'm sure she felt the same feelings I did. Since that last sunset, since Rhodes had dipped into the sea, the world for me had been a black and white place. There were shades of gray, of course, and tinges of bright red in my memories. But little else.

And now, here before our eyes, the world filled with color again. As far as we could see, our mental oceans of gray were replaced with fields of yellow, blue, and a hundred other wonderful colors. Sima turned her face toward me.

"L'chaim," she said.

"L'chaim," I replied, and felt myself smiling.

At the hospital in Ystad, I was given my own room. Though simply furnished, it was clean and full of light. It even had its own bathroom. I was put to bed the moment I arrived and didn't rise for two days. I was still too weak to walk.

My window looked out on a clean, landscaped park, and over the days I was in that room, the sight of that peaceful place did much to heal my spirit. I also had my own nurse, a wonderful Swedish woman named Ingrid. She reminded me of Grandmama and was about the same age she would have been. Ingrid didn't speak much, mainly because we did not share a common language. But she was nearly always with me. Perhaps Ingrid's presence was a planned part of my care and recuperation. This change from black and white to color, from inhumanity to humanity, from indignity to respect, occurred over the space of only a few days. It was almost too much to accept, and it became easy to wonder if any of it had really happened. But I wouldn't have been there in the condition I was in if it hadn't really occurred. The two extremes were, at times, too contradictory for my healing mind. The need to heal did not want to confront the actions of the past that had caused the damage. So what was real, and what was fantasy? I still had no news of my family. Time had no meaning to me, and I felt as though I should surely have heard by now if anyone was alive. And what she couldn't tell me, she showed me. As the days would pass, as I would slowly regain an appetite and the ability to walk, Ingrid would take me out into that park to enjoy the tulips and smell the smells of spring. She would teach me how to knit and would bring yarn and knitting needles to my room. She smiled at me, and after a time, I found the ability to smile back.

Dr. Soderlund, a tall, impeccably dressed physician, came to examine me at least twice daily those first few weeks. Like Ingrid, he was a calm, knowing, reassuring presence whenever he visited.

"Are you able to sleep, Laura?"

"No. No, not very well."

"Why?"

"I have memories."

"What kind of memories? Do you mean memories of the camps?"

I shook my head. "Not usually, no. I have memories I can't remember."

He looked confused. "I don't understand, Laura."

I didn't say anything for a moment. I could feel myself struggling to maintain my composure without tears. "In the dark, when I am alone here, I close my eyes and try to see my family. I try so hard to remember their faces, to remember what my mother's smile felt like."

"You can't see them?"

My eyes welled with tears. "No. I see only shadows in my mind." I began to sob. "They must all be dead. I can't remember what they look like. I can't hear their voices. I can't. . . . There are only shadows."

He touched my arm gently but said nothing. He got up from where he had been sitting on the bed to speak with me and returned moments later with a small glass of water.

"Here. This will help you sleep, Laura. There's a sleeping powder mixed in this. You need to sleep and relax as much as you can so you can get better."

And sleep I did. For two days there were no shadows in my mind. There were no worries about whether my family had survived. There was no wondering whether I would. There was only the blackness of deep sleep and the occasional sense of those soft, cool sheets that blanketed me.

I awoke to bright sunlight streaming through the window, and I was alone. Ingrid had probably thought I would sleep longer and had taken a well-deserved break from her watchfulness. The warmth of the sun felt wonderful, and the rest had done much to provide a little strength and improve my mental state. Cautiously, I sat up in bed. Carefully, I pulled back the sheets and put my feet on the floor. Slowly, ever so slowly, I stood next to the bed, feeling dizzy as my body adjusted to what had become an unaccustomed position. But I didn't fall. After a few moments, I began walking haltingly toward the bathroom.

I caught my breath as the bathroom door opened before me. As I stood there, holding myself erect in the doorway, I realized without any doubt that what had happened to me was real. I closed my eyes and saw the gaunt, hollow faces of the dead, staring that blank, final stare of utter futility. I could feel myself losing my balance amid this sea of death and gray, foul, leatherlike flesh. I opened my eyes and let out a little cry. Before me, those wide, hollow eyes of the barracks' dead stared back at me with cognition. Before me, my own reflection stared back from the bathroom mirror.

Ingrid must have heard my cry, for she rushed into the room. With a little gasp, she put her arms around me as I wept. We just stood there for a time; I was horrified at what I had become, she was consoling and strong. I peered sadly at the mirror from her embrace. Through my tears, I saw the agonized, tragic countenance of myself. It frightened me terribly. How close I had come to joining the dead!

I don't remember much about food, except that one of my first meals consisted of a little spaghetti with sugar on it. How odd, I thought, but in retrospect the sugar may have been a contrivance simply to provide a source of energy for me. Throughout those first days, Ingrid and Dr. Soderlund encouraged me to eat whatever I could manage, and the hospital staff tried to provide foods I was accustomed to, like that sugared pasta they called spaghetti.

I had been in that little room for almost three weeks. Three weeks of sleep, slowly increasing meals, and Dr. Soderlund's daily conversations. For her part, Ingrid cared for me like an elderly matriarch doting on her first grandchild. She was always there, it seemed, and though our words were few, our relationship became close. Slowly, she taught me a little Swedish, and I taught her a bit of Italian. And as the days passed, we would sit in the room together for hours, with only the occasional click of knitting needles, as beautiful sweaters and shawls materialized from our occupation. With few words but most meaningful actions, Ingrid had become my guardian and my family. The reward for her constant care was the slow return of my strength and the even slower return of a degree of emotional stability.

Still, I wondered about my family and if they were alive. Why hadn't I heard anything? Even though I knew some had perished, I clung to the hope that I had somehow been wrong. But with each day, hope became more difficult. I lashed out at myself at times, angrily believing that I had been duped about the promises of the Red Cross. Other times I retreated into depression, thinking that everyone was dead, thinking that chance had cruelly dictated that I be the only one left. But in spite of myself, I stubbornly clung to whatever strands of hope I could muster from my consciousness. It was just that, as time passed, the strands were becoming thinner and thinner. My father and mother, after all, were just shadows in the dark, horrible, nighttime worlds my mind created. As the days passed, even the shadows began to fade, leaving emptiness in their place.

But with the help of those who cared for me, my physical and psychological healing continued despite my depression. Dr. Soderlund, for example, spoke often to me about anti-Semitism and the camps, and he even arranged tests of my reactions to sudden reminders of the past. On one occasion, Ingrid and I had sat near the window, and she had pointed out to me a "Nazi" walking in the park. On another, when I first had been allowed out of the room to walk by myself in the park, the same man appeared. In both cases, my reaction had been abject fear. I had nearly fallen from the window seat when Ingrid said that word. I found a way to actually run when I saw the man face to face. I believe that Dr. Soderlund knew what my reactions would be in such situations. What he was evaluating was the depth of my reaction. Would I faint? Would I scream at the sight of a German? Would I flail at him in rage, weak as I was? The good doctor and Ingrid needed to know, so that they could understand what needed to be done to enable me to cope with the world of freedom. Though their methods may have seemed deceptive and cruel at the time, they were physically harmless. Except for the sleeping powder and medication for my diseases, my recovery was free of drugs. Moreover, Ingrid was always nearby to provide a loving, guiding embrace after such travails. In time, her strength gave me the strength to face the past as I realized my future. In a very real sense, she and Dr. Soderlund took the role of the wise man in my story. At this crucial time of redemption, they would not let me forget my past. The difficulty was, there was nothing there for me except horror. The horror buried Rhodes and the beauty of my life there; it was smothered like the faceless shadows of my family.

In spite of all this inner turmoil, my strength had begun to return, and the weaknesses associated with my disease began to fade. I was still very thin, but no longer skeletal. My eyes still had dark circles around them, but they no longer appeared wide and staring like those of the dead. Unfortunately, the better I got, the more difficult living became. There had still been no word of my family, and I could sense my thin strands of hope were breaking. I began to believe they were all dead.

I had been in Ystad for a little over a month when Dr. Soderlund apparently decided I was well enough to be relocated. I don't remember saying good-bye to him or to Ingrid, and I had had little contact with any other patients or staff at the hospital. All at once, a young man named Kummelnes appeared in my room, helped me pack a few belongings, and took me to Stockholm. There, I was to be placed in a facility for displaced people, a temporary home while I completed my recuperation. A temporary home while I wondered if I had a home or family to return to.

The facility itself was far different from that in Ystad. It was a modern, large chalet of sorts, with none of the doctors and nurses I had been accustomed to. I missed Ingrid immediately, but my sadness was quickly replaced by the presence of other survivors. They seemed to be everywhere and from every corner of the world. There were no restrictions imposed by the doctors and nurses here. We could talk with each other as we pleased. We could come and go about the streets of Stockholm as we wished. Most of all, we were free to learn again what freedom was like.

I met Sima again in Stockholm, and over time, I became friends with several other survivors my age. Except in occasional one-on-one conversation, we seldom spoke of the camps. It was as if we all knew that the experiences we had shared, the things we had seen, might horribly upset the others, might trigger a fearful response that would shatter a fragile existence. For the most part, we didn't want to talk about it. We wanted to look forward, not back, to that too-recent bestial time. Nonetheless, there were moments during those months in Stockholm when the Holocaust would burst forth upon us like a vicious serpent.

Benjamin was a young man from Salonika, Greece. Serious, handsome, and intelligent, he seemed like many of us to be preoccupied with a terrible secret. And though he laughed and smiled and talked freely as we wandered the streets, there would be times for all of us when the secret had to be told. His was with me one late afternoon while we sat in a Stockholm park. He had noticed my tattoo and mentioned that the number seemed familiar to him.

"Were you in Auschwitz?" He almost whispered the word.

I looked down and whispered back. I heard myself speak the word in that same silent voice we had used so much in the camps. "Yes."

"Where? What part of the camp were you in?"

"Birkenau. Barrack 20 and Barrack 7," I winced.

Benjamin said nothing for a very long time. I looked at him briefly as we walked among the trees and the song of the birds.

"I worked in the crematorium in Auschwitz, Laura."

I stopped. I stared in his eyes. There was such a look of sadness there. Such a hollowness. I touched his hand, and he took mine, shaking.

"I, I can still hear them screaming, Laura. I can still hear them crying out every night in my nightmares."

I pulled away from him. I took several quick steps backward, almost in a bolt. "No. No. No. I do not want to hear! No. Please."

Benjamin stopped speaking and looked at me as if dumbfounded. I had put my hands to my ears and stood there a few feet from him, shaking my head. I did not want to hear his secret. I did not want to hear because what he had already said was almost too much to bear. If there were screams in his memory, then the bodies he placed in the ovens were still living. If there were cries of terror, they were of those who felt their flesh being burned from their limbs. I struggled to regain my composure. My breath came in quick, short gasps for a time. My eyes stared at him in utter fear for those who had cried out to him.

Benjamin looked away from me. "I tried not to look in their faces, Laura. I might have seen a friend, or my father." He began to cry. "I am so afraid. Please, Laura. I can't tell anyone of this. I can't. They will accuse me of being a murderer." He put his face in his hands, weeping openly.

"I don't know how I will live with this secret. I don't know how I can live with this guilt."

I did not rush to hold Benjamin in my arms, though a part of me told me I must. Slowly, I walked the few feet to where he cried and again took his hand in mine.

"Benjamin," I soothed, "You did nothing wrong from within yourself, and you must remember that. We are victims, Benjamin. Victims! You did not choose to murder at the crematorium, you were forced to," I sighed. "I know that, Benjamin, and all of us know about the sonderkommando. We know you had no choice in what you did, except to die yourself."

Benjamin looked back at me, his eyes overflowing with tears. "Then why do they torment me so? Why do they all scream back at me in my nightmares?"

I rolled his fingers gently in my hand. "Because you are human, Benjamin. Because you are a human who had to do inhuman acts," I sighed. "I know that's not a very good answer. But it is a true one."

That evening, I found myself alone with my thoughts. Like a maddening wound freshly reopened, the events of the day filled my mind with fear. Was Father one of those whom Benjamin threw on the flames? Did Mother somehow survive the gas, only to be incinerated alive? Could anyone from my family have survived such double torture? I closed my eyes, and once again fought back tears. We were all so alone, so incredibly trapped by what had befallen us. For Benjamin, the guilt associated with what he had been forced to do now plagued him. To remember it was to relive the unimaginable. To forget was unforgivable. To live with the Holocaust, one had to speak of it. There was no way for any of us to break this vicious cycle of pain and fear. Only the dulling effect of time, and time alone, would make our lives bearable existences once again. In our own way, each of us would find a means to live with it over time. If we could not, we would die.

It had been three months since I had been liberated. I slept no better this night than my first night in Ystad.

How strange the world had become for those of us who had survived. Our existence was torn between guilt and justification—yet such controversy was, by necessity, internal to each of us. Our emotions were constantly in turmoil. On the one hand, we would be dealing with utter depression within ourselves. On the other, we would find moments of contentment and, sometimes, joy. That these contrasts occurred in such close timeframes to one another was difficult and, for some, impossible to contend with. From the depths of our loneliness and the recent memories it brought, one could find one's self atop a crest of joy, triggered by something as simple as Dr. Soderlund's respectful knock at my door in Ystad. We had all lived in the utter depths of despair for so long that such joys were met with suspicion, but for a different reason than one would expect. Life in Sweden was a series of rapid emotional precipices. The trouble was, we learned very quickly that we had no emotional balance. We could fall off the precipice as quickly as we had been lifted to it.

The morning after my talk with Benjamin, I had eaten breakfast and was sitting with Sima on the lawn outside the chalet. It seemed these days that most of us preferred the outdoors, weather permitting, than being inside. The sight of green lawns and flowers was something we had missed, something that still seemed new and refreshing to us. Of course, I dared not speak to Sima of my conversation with Benjamin. I dared not talk of the turmoil the subject had prompted within me, or my sleepless night. I had, after all, promised Benjamin I would keep his secret. More importantly, I knew that if I spoke of it, I might initiate in Sima a similar recurrence of fear and remembrance such as I had experienced the previous evening. So we spoke of other things. We talked about the handsome men we saw in the chalet or about the streets. We talked about the birds we heard and the summer flowers in the parks. Sima was reminiscing about our first train ride and the tulips we'd seen, when Kummelnes came running to us from the chalet.

"Laura! There is a telephone call for you."

I looked back at him, confused. He stood a few feet from me, panting from the run. "Telephone? For me?"

"Yes. For Laura Varon. Come, Laura."

I hesitated. "Come, Laura, come. Don't be afraid."

Kummelnes showed me to the room where the receiver sat on a small table. I was afraid. Who would call me? Would I hear what I feared most, that I was the only one left? I picked up the handset. "Hello?"

The voice on the other end of the line came in Italian. "Hello. This is the Italian Consulate. Is this Miss Laura Varon?"

"Yes, this is Laura Varon."

"We have a telegram from a Mr. Nissim Cohen in the Belgian Congo. Shall I read the telegram?"

I screamed. A loud, long scream of joy.

"Yes! Yes! Read it please!"

"I am trying to locate anyone from the Isle of Rhodes with the last names of Cohen, Varon, or Hasson. Stop. Please advise at earliest if persons fitting description are found. Stop. Signed, Nissim Cohen. Stop. End of message, Miss Varon."

I was crying uncontrollably. My hands shook from the adrenaline that coursed through me. My tears fell freely from atop the precipice.

"Miss Varon?"

I sobbed.

"Miss Varon? Is there anything you wish to tell Mr. Cohen?"

"Yes, yes," I blurted. "Tell him I am alive."

Some four thousand miles from Stockholm, a missionary who knew Uncle Nissim had been listening to the radio. In an unrelated news story, the missionary heard that some survivors from Bergen-Belsen had been taken to Sweden for recuperation. Fortunately, the missionary knew that Uncle Nissim had been writing letters and contacting consulates in every country where survivors were known to be. He went to Uncle and told him about Sweden. Had he contacted the consulate there?

Within an hour, Uncle Nissim's telegram was being read to me. I was the only one in the family he had located.

Uncle Nissim immediately began sending me letters, little gifts, and money for anything I might need. And within a fairly short time, he had arranged for me to leave the chalet to stay with a Jewish family elsewhere in the city. The authorities had told him that I was in a survivors' camp. Uncle Nissim did not want me living in a "camp" of any kind. With some difficulty, he had made arrangements for me to live with the Greenbergs until I was strong enough to leave Sweden and travel to Italy.

I don't remember saying good-bye to Sima or Benjamin or Kummelnes or any of the other friends I had made since coming to Stockholm. I believe I had developed an aversion to parting that prevented me from remembering the circumstances of leaving places and people that had been a comfort to me. To this day, good-byes are still painful. I believe it's because none of us wanted to face departure and the feelings associated with it. If we never said good-bye, we could at least avoid falling off yet another emotional precipice.

Mr. and Mrs. Greenberg lived in a quiet neighborhood on the outskirts of Stockholm. He was an admiral in the Swedish navy, and Mrs. Greenberg was very active in the synagogue and community affairs. They had one daughter, Dagma, who was 22 and full of life. I was immediately attracted to her spirit. She was athletic, active, and well educated. She was a person who enjoyed taking responsibility, enjoyed making decisions, and expected no less from those around her. What a contrast she was from those I had been accustomed to! Dagma bore none of the scars and deep emotional wounds we survivors carried every moment. She had no fear like the fear we could muster in an instant. She embraced life for what it should have been for all of us.

Yet Dagma understood that I was as yet incapable of the quick decisiveness with which she pursued everything. She knew I was still emotionally and physically frail. Her response was to shelter and care for me with an intelligence and maturity that belied her years.

At the same time, my spirits were improving with every message from Uncle Nissim. Among his many encouraging letters and gifts from the Congo, he had sent me a telegram advising that he had located Uncle Rahamin in Rome. Though our joy in finding him was tempered somewhat by the fact that we had found no one else these many months, I was, nonetheless, bolstered by the news. I was still thin, but there was reason to live again. I was not alone.

Dagma and her parents seemed to take me everywhere in Stockholm, but my excursions with Dagma alone were the most special. We would spend hours together frequenting the little cafes that dotted the city. I would watch Dagma's dark blue eyes, so full of life, as she talked excitedly about college or any of a dozen other subjects. She was showing me life again. She was making me live it once again. Though my nightmares still haunted me, there were moments with Dagma as sweet as the wonderful hot chocolate the cafes served us. There were moments when, despite the language and the climate, despite the many strange ways of Sweden, I was reminded of home.

And as those days and weeks with the Greenbergs passed, our bonds became stronger and more intimate. Alexander Greenberg, Dagma's father, enlisted his many resources to try to find word of my family. Mrs. Greenberg was a smiling, warm, constant support to all of us together. She was a most special, sophisticated woman. I imagined at times that Mother would have been much like her, had she been gifted with wealth and education. People who believe in God say that everything happens for His reason. If that is true, then

His reason must have been to give me redemption through the Greenbergs. Together, we found ways to fill in many of those canyons of depression. I began to feel something I doubted I would ever feel again—a part of a family.

But even the most touching, special moments were not always easy. After dinner one night, the conversation with the Greenberg family became strangely serious. Dagma told me that they all cared very deeply for me. With the nodding assent of her parents, she then said that, if my family were found not to have survived the camps, they would like to adopt me as their own. It was a most special, intimate moment of love, and I was deeply touched. But at the same time, I was alarmed to hear mention that perhaps my immediate family had not survived. I was, after all, still clinging to hope and belief that, somehow, at least some of them lived. I could not yet accept, I could not yet believe, that they were dead.

I got up from my seat at the table and walked around to where Dagma sat. There were tears in my eyes and I hugged her. "I love you all, but let's wait a little while. If I hear they have died, or if I never find them, then I will be so honored to be your sister." I looked at Mr. and Mrs. Greenberg. ". . . and your daughter."

It is difficult to appreciate how much freedom means until you live without it. But freedom brought with it choices I was unaccustomed to making: Choices between staying indoors and wandering the streets of Stockholm; choices between a wonderful, vibrant family and one that might be dead; choices between belief and disbelief.

I suppose I still believed in God those days in Stockholm, but I, like many, held a deep, seething anger that He had betrayed us. How could I love a God who had forsaken us to the God of Chance, who had permitted babies to be ripped apart in front of my eyes, who had allowed those gruesome stacks of His people to accumulate? I suppose I still believed, but that belief was tempered by the perception that God had far more human qualities than the rabbis in Rhodes had led me to believe. God made mistakes. God was indifferent to those who loved Him. God owed me.

For those of us who still believed in God, liberation from the camps was seldom filled with prayers of thanksgiving. If we even thought of Him at the time, it was usually not to praise Him for allowing us to live, for allowing us to exist in a world of nightmares, guilt, and unbelievable loss. More typically, our thoughts centered around a simple question that was asked thousands upon thousands of times: "How could You let this happen to us?"

I suppose I believed in God. In fact, there were times in the camps when I desperately held to belief in His existence. As I sat there against the barrack wall, staring at the stinking, wide-eyed remains of my friends, feeling the lice suck at me, I hoped against hope that God would appear before me. I desperately wished He would take form there, in those few feet between me and the bodies, so I could have spat in His face.

Still, there are things stronger than such despair, if one had the strength to recall them. In Rhodes, God was a fundamental part of my life, as wondrous as the sweet sounds of the *shema* that drifted through the streets, as intimate as those magical evenings under the *succoh*. As I wondered and worried about my family, I remembered when life was full of light. I remembered the warmth of Mother's arms, the magic of Grandmama's smile, the morals of Father's stories. God was the glue that held together our family, the fabric that wove together our community, the substance of our traditions and customs.

For me, life without God was meaningless. And though the Nazis had drastically altered my relationship with Him, I clung to the traditions of which He was so basic a part. Despite what He had allowed to happen to me, I realized I needed Him still, for without Him, there would be no substance to my life. I decided that Hitler, wherever he was, would not have the pleasure of seeing one more Jew become something less.

And so it was that, as the High Holy Days approached in September 1945, I willingly attended synagogue with Dagma and her parents. I didn't know exactly what I might say to God, whether I would be angry with Him or somehow thank Him or talk to Him at all. But I would participate in the rituals. I would sing the songs and listen in awe to the magnificent chants of the cantor. It was tradition. It was me.

It had been over a year since I'd seen the candles lit in synagogue or a rabbi read from the Torah. It was like home, like the thousand times I'd recited the *shema* or watched the men below me pray. They were like bees on the honeycomb, all humming their Hebrew in wonderful discord. Their heads with yamulkas swayed back and forth or side to side with the rhythm of their individual prayers, and talits, those ancient, sacred signs of Jewish identity, covered their shoulders or heads in the white-and-blue stripes of the hive. Though the accents were different, that same ancient Hebrew that had linked us all for thousands of years now once again resounded in my ears. I thought of all the stories of persecution I'd heard as a child, of the exile in Babylon, the destruction of the Temple, the dispersion of all of us to the four corners of the earth. And now there was this new persecution. A thousand years from now, would what we had just endured be remembered as just another footnote to history, just another moment of terror in a string of hundreds? How many more Lauras would see what I had seen because of what we believed or how we lived or what we strove to do with our lives? At one time or another, we survivors would be faced with asking ourselves the same question. If God had a reason for everything, was ours to ensure that the world knew of the Holocaust? To ensure, somehow, that it should never happen again? And if that were true, how might I do my part? How might I do my part without driving myself mad? It was that same dilemma creeping back again. To remain silent was to allow the demons of guilt and anger to gnaw away at your consciousness; to talk was to relive the pain every time you did. For me, there would be no closure, no personal completion of the butchery we call the Holocaust. I am a survivor, yes, but I am imprinted forever with the nightmare.

I thought of Father and how much he loved to bid for the honor and the right to place the silver bells on the Torah. As they replaced them now, I heard their gentle, twinkling chime. Were they sounding for Father's memory? Would I soon say the *Kaddish* for my family? Dear God, you must let them be alive. Please. Let me see them again in this life. Let me know I am not alone. . . .

Dagma looked at me in some alarm but said nothing. I must have talked with Him and prayed to Him for the better part of a half-hour, but Dagma said nothing until long after services were completed.

"You frightened me, Laura. Your lips were moving and there was perspiration on your forehead. You rocked back and forth and it seemed as if you were about to fly away, right there in the synagogue. If it is not too personal, can I ask what you were praying so intently for?"

I looked at her for a moment before speaking. We were sitting on the front steps of the house. "I prayed for answers. I prayed to know how I might escape from what boils inside me. I asked God to let me see my family again."

After that, nothing more was said about adoption until, standing with the telegram in hand, I told Dagma that Uncle Nissim had located my brothers. Joseph and Asher had been found in Bologna, Italy. They, at least, had found the strength and the means to do as Mother had asked.

"I am so very happy for you, Laura. At least we know that part of your family is alive." She touched my arm. "But I am sad, too. You will probably leave us now. I will probably not have the chance to live with you as my sister." Dagma's eyes burned into mine. It was a question, not a statement. She looked at me for the slightest sign she might be wrong. I said nothing. I could say nothing. My feelings for Dagma and her family paled in comparison to my love for my own. That was how it should be, and we both knew it.

But I was still battling the emotional precipices and canyons of being a survivor. I was overjoyed to know that my brothers had survived and were, apparently, well. Despite Dagma's sadness, I realized at last that I was not alone. There was a chance, at least, that I had something of a family left after all.

Still, there was that canyon to fall into. Barely two days after hearing about Joseph and Asher, Dagma's uncle found that my mother, father, and the others who had gone to the left that day we entered Auschwitz were on an official list of the deceased. I had hoped but now I was forced to believe. And in the instantaneous depression that followed, I found myself alone in the synagogue.

Whether it was God's help or the natural evolution of my recovery I will never know, but my depression over the death of my parents left me as soon as I left the synagogue. I had thanked God for the lives of my brothers. I had said the *Kaddish* for my mother and father. And strangely, I had listened to the words I spoke:

". . . May the One who causes peace to reign in the high heavens, let peace descend on us, on all Israel, and all the world, and let us say: Amen. May the Source of peace send peace to all who mourn, and comfort to all who are bereaved. Amen."

There was a peace in knowing the fate that had befallen my mother and father, Grandmama, Auntie Diana, and the little children

Jaco and Baby Mattie. I had seen them go to the left that day in Auschwitz, and I later came to know what that meant. But I had, like so many others, hoped against hope that they had survived. Now, at last, I knew with certainty that they had not. Though today I understand that my uncertainty was contrived, at that time I realized that knowing was much better than not knowing, even if knowing meant the worst. I at least knew I had some family left. I could at least try to heal now.

I felt a certain peace as I walked back to the Greenbergs' that night. Still, there were many others I had not heard about. There were aunts and uncles and friends like Jaco and Salvo I wished I knew of. And there was Stella. I shivered in the cool of the evening, coughing a bit as I neared the street where the Greenbergs lived.

While my time those days was consumed with healing and determining the fate of my family, there were others who were consumed with trying to find me. After several failures, Laurina had finally found my whereabouts through the Red Cross. I had not seen or heard from her since we had been separated in Malmo, and I was most surprised when she telephoned me at the Greenbergs'.

Laurina had recovered quickly from her physical ailments and had been living in Stockholm since she was released from the field hospital in Malmo. At first, she had found support from the Jewish community in Stockholm. Now she worked as a nanny, caring for the children of a well-to-do Italian car dealer and his wife.

But while Laurina had not had the physical difficulties I did, her emotional burdens were greater. Laurina was the sole survivor of a family of five. Her mother and father had perished in the gas chambers; her brother Leon and sister Mary had both died in the labor camps. Still, she seemed to be doing well. "I'm doing the best I can with this, you know?" she told me. "I have to accept life as it is now. I have to live."

After that first call, Laurina and I often met to talk and visit the parks and cafes around Stockholm. I would tell her about Dagma and show her some of the places the Greenbergs had taken me. She would talk to me about being a nanny for two small children and how silly she felt having to wear a nanny's uniform. I loved meeting with my most special friend, and I loved our walks and conversation. Still, there was something missing from our talks, something that at first I couldn't quite put my finger on. It only occurred to me after I very quickly and reluctantly told her about my mother and father.

Laurina and I talked and laughed about everything that occupied our everyday lives. We shared our dreams and giggled over men and laughingly gobbled the wonderful pastries and chocolates we could find in the cafes. But we never reminisced. Except in passing, we never spoke of the Holocaust. We never spoke of Rhodes.

As the days passed, what had appeared to be a light cold seemed to stay with me longer than it should have. I passed it off without concern, even though Dagma and Laurina both had mentioned my cough. But after an evening out with Dagma and some of her friends, I began to feel feverish on the walk home, and I eventually collapsed after facing the warmth of the house. Mrs. Greenberg rushed me to the hospital where, after an extensive examination and X-rays, the doctors found I had double pneumonia.

So just as it seemed that my emotional precipices and canyons were leveling out, my physical problems intervened with a vengeance. The doctors told Mrs. Greenberg and Dagma that I had suffered a relapse of sorts because I had undertaken too much activity too early in my recovery from typhus. I was placed in critical care for the next several days.

The Greenbergs, of course, immediately notified Uncle Nissim of my condition. From that moment onward, he was in constant contact with the doctors, and he got updates on my condition on a daily basis. Laurina was devastated to hear of my illness. I remember her sitting by my bed, holding my hand, and tearfully telling me that I simply had to pull through this sickness. "You are my only sister, Laura. You are my only family. Everyone else is dead. You must get better, Laura. You must get better. I don't want to lose you, too."

Within a week I was moved to a room with four other girls during the day, but I had to be returned to critical care for observation at night. I was still seriously ill, but I seemed to be improving steadily. It wasn't very long before I could talk to some of the other girls while I was in their room.

One of them was Llia Vytautas, a refugee from Lithuania who had escaped just before the Germans had overrun her country. She was about 40 years old and had been in the hospital for some weeks for treatment of a heart condition. But there was something special about Llia, something that gave her a warmth and understanding of my plight that extended far beyond words. She knew I had survived the camps. Perhaps, I thought, she had survived some similar holocaust of her own. She reminded me of Marushka because she had an inner confidence, a sense of herself, that permitted her to give to others freely. Llia gave me warm conversation and, after a time, a gift. It was a silver spoon, emblazoned with her family's coat of arms. It was a special honor to me, for Llia had given me a part of her heritage, a heritage that extended back to Lithuanian royalty in the Middle Ages.

After two weeks I was allowed to get out of bed, walk through the hospital halls, and sit outside my room. It was like the first time I got out of bed in Ystad, like learning to walk all over again. Still, within a couple of days, I was able to wander the halls comfortably, and my conversations with Llia were now supplemented with small trips to the nurses' stations and waiting rooms for magazines or newspapers. I was at last beginning to truly recover from my pneumonia— or so I thought.

It had only been a few days since I'd been ambulatory when a searing pain struck my chest. It happened so suddenly that I remembered wondering if this was what it felt like to be shot. Wincing with the pain, I simply sat on a couch in the hallway until a nurse noticed my condition. Within minutes, I was back in bed with my doctor listening intently through a stethoscope to the sounds in my chest. He looked at me in some alarm.

"I don't understand how this has happened, but you have pleurisy, Laura. You have developed water in your chest cavity. You're going to have to stay in bed again."

Of course, that was only a small part of my treatment. I had needles inserted in my chest and my back to draw out the liquid. I had countless X-rays to ensure that, as my pleurisy improved, I did not regress to tuberculosis. I had several medications for both the condition itself and for the pain that went with it. For the first several days after this setback, I could barely move and could not lie on either side without excruciating pain.

The doctors said that my apparent proclivity for illness was due to the fact that, even after nearly a year, I was still in weak physical condition from my ordeal in the camps. But I knew better. I believe to this day that Nature tries to step in to ensure survival if the conscious cannot deal with the anguish of life. While certainly my stay with the Greenbergs and Dagma was helping my recovery, the extremes of my emotional existence were fast becoming too much to bear. Uncle Nissim had found me, and Benjamin had thrown the still-living on the fires of Auschwitz. My brothers were alive, but nearly all my other relatives were dead. I had found a way to believe in God again, but He still kept Stella's fate a secret from me.

Perhaps it had been my renewed thoughts of her that had tipped the scales and made me sick. I had long since deeply buried my guilt over Stella amid the struggles of survival in the camps and, particularly, my concerns over the fates of others. Stella had become my deepest secret, my personal Benjamin-like horror. I dared not think of her, or even conjure her name from memory, lest I begin anew that crazed anxiety over another unkept promise to Mother.

I was to spend another full month in the hospital amid what seemed like constant X-rays and continuing instructions to rest. Uncle Nissim, watchful from afar as always, was still in almost daily contact with the doctors. He wanted me to come to the Belgian Congo to live, but the doctors were telling him I had a good deal of time to spend in Sweden before I was well enough to make such a journey. They couldn't say exactly how long that might be, but when I was finally released from the hospital in February, Uncle Nissim sent me enough money to last for about six months.

Laurina had visited me daily while I was in the hospital and was nearly as frequent a visitor when I returned to recuperate at the Greenbergs. Unfortunately, her presence there soon strained my relationships with Dagma and particularly Mr. and Mrs. Greenberg. It wasn't long before they were discouraging me from spending time with Laurina, and I believe they felt her nature to be too liberal for their liking. They were not unkind to Laurina, but neither did they appreciate my closeness to her. Perhaps they felt she would somehow take advantage of me, and they worried that I would be a willing pawn. Dagma once said I should spend my time with people of better stature. Mr. and Mrs. Greenberg were more subtle. They said it was time for me to expand my friendships to others. They felt I was far too consumed with my relationship with Laurina.

At the time, they were probably right. But neither Dagma nor her parents understood, or could understand, what Laurina and I had been through together. Certainly they knew there was a special bond between us, but no amount of discussion could bring comprehension of the depth of our connection. We had seen the unbelievable, had bid farewell to our way of life and families, had kept each other alive through the most bitter existence imaginable. But more than that, we had come to understand each other's deepest emotions, darkest fears, and fundamental spirituality during our time in the camps. Together, we had thrown the bodies on the piles, she grasping under the arms and I holding the ankles. Forged in those moments, the fundamental links between us could never be broken, irrespective of the good intentions of those who might intervene.

And so it was that within a fairly short time, Laurina and I decided to get an apartment together. Uncle Nissim objected strenuously at first, but he assented when I told him of Laurina's and my relationship. He only wanted my happiness, he said, and to be assured I was not taking on more than my physical condition could stand. I told him that Laurina had almost become like a nanny to me; we had even discussed her leaving her job to care for the apartment we were to live in. Uncle Nissim's response was to approve our apartment venture and to provide enough money for Laurina to leave her job.

The Greenbergs, of course, were deeply saddened by my apparent rejection of all their love and care. They had provided well for me, even to the extent of paying for my needs and managing the money Uncle Nissim had sent previously on my behalf. Why, then, should I simply walk out on them when they had given me so much?

The truth be known, I believe that my relationship with Laurina had little to do with it. I was a young woman who had, to this point, been controlled in some way all my life. Mother and Father had had control before I was old enough to accept much responsibility for myself. Hitler and his henchmen had controlled my life over a period of time when I should have been first exploring my freedoms. The doctors had controlled me through all my illness, practically the full year since I had been liberated. Little wonder, then, that I bolted away from the Greenbergs at the slightest hint that they might control much more than my money. I had most politely rejected the control implied in their adoption of me. I had overreacted when they had attempted to control my relationship with Laurina. Regardless of their obvious good intentions, I was struggling mightily to break free of the chains of my past and any manipulation of my present. I was, at last, rebelling. I was finally having the opportunity to do something most teenagers do, but from the perspective of a young adult. When the opportunity arose through Laurina, I seized it tenaciously. At last I would be able to experience the results of my own decisions in my own time. At last I would be able to take responsibility freely.

Dagma helped me find the apartment and even helped me move my belongings. She only told me, "Be careful, Laura," when, through tears, she said good-bye from the door of the apartment. Though I know I hurt them deeply, I hope and believe they found the wisdom to understand my lust for freedom at the time. I will never forget them. For what they did for me, I will be indebted forever. I only wish that, at the time, I had had the wisdom to handle our parting differently.

But what one sows, one reaps. Within a month of moving into the apartment together, Laurina introduced me to her fiancé. He was a young, intelligent, mild-mannered man named Severino. He was also a Polish Jew.

At the time, I suppose what I needed most was to be needed. I had been abused, mentally and physically tortured, and, most of all, made to feel worthless in the camps. As a result, I believe that the special relationship Laurina and I had developed was based on our mutual need for survival and on a more fundamental need to have value to someone else. Unfortunately, I had made a transition of that same need to Sweden. I was for all intent and purposes alone, and Laurina represented a singular emotional safe haven for me. She understood me, and I could need her without fear of rejection. I understood her, and I needed desperately to be needed—to feel valuable to someone.

Little wonder then that I felt Laurina had betrayed me. She had obviously had a relationship with Severino for some time, but she had never mentioned it until now. She didn't need me as I thought she did. There was someone else she could rely on beside me, and I knew I could not compete. After meeting Severino, I left the apartment angry, resentful, and feeling terribly alone.

But I also knew how much Laurina was like me. Uncle Nissim had been checking with the doctors frequently, and Laurina knew it would not be long before I would leave for Italy to be with my brothers and Uncle Rahamin. Though I will never know for sure, it is likely that she entered into a relationship with Severino as a guarantee that she would have someone to need her, and that she could need, after I was gone. And though my links to family were precarious, hers were nonexistent. At that time, Laurina had no one except me and, now, Severino. My resentment faded quickly when I considered the facts. Laurina was doing what I very likely would have done were our roles reversed. She was simply ensuring that someone would be there to hold her hand, to talk to her, to comfort her, when she awoke from the terrible nightmares we all shared.

Two weeks later, Laurina and Severino drove me to the airport. Our conversation was full of her plans for the future and my trepidation at flying for the first time. We continued this small talk through our arrival, baggage check, and walk to the gate where I would board the plane. We both hated good-byes. We minimized this departure with our idle chatter, at least until I had finally turned from her to walk the last few feet to the doorway onto the tarmac.

"Laura."

I turned back to see Laurina's eyes were filled with tears.

"Do you remember our pact?"

It was the first time either of us had spoken directly about the camps.

"I will never forget our pact."

She paused for a moment, staring sadly into my eyes. "I think that maybe we should still keep that pact, Laura, even though we survived."

I was confused. "What do you mean?"

Laurina took both my hands in hers. She stammered. "I, I think maybe we did die, Laura. At least that part of us that was innocent. I think someday we need to tell everyone what happened. I think we need to tell everyone how we died." She looked up for a second, and tears now dribbled down her cheeks. "Someday, Laura, we must tell the story. Someday when we can endure reliving it."

The emotion welled up in me, as with, my lips quivering, I kissed her. "I love you."

She said nothing. She just nodded her head. I turned and nearly ran to the airplane.

7.

REUNION
_____

I WAS AT LAST well enough to keep one of my promises to Mother. Though I know she would have understood my delay, there was still a very real satisfaction in being able to tell myself that I had honored my pledge to her. And while the guilt in failing to care for Stella still plagued me, I chose to believe in the remote possibility she might still be alive. If she were, my decision to leave her in the infirmary would have been vindicated in spite of Mother's instructions.

But in my mind, there was little likelihood Stella would be any-where but Italy if she were alive. She, too, had heard Mother's ad-monition and would have struck out for an Italian city, Milan if possible, if she were liberated. That being the case, I knew that returning to Italy was not just a part of keeping a promise; it was the one place where I could do the most good in trying to find her. I resolved to be Uncle Nissim's arms as he continued to look for Stella. I would peer in any doorway, visit any city, talk to any stranger who might know of her fate. I resolved to be as much help to Uncle Rahamin, Joseph, and Asher as I could. There was little altruism in this; finding anyone in the family would help the emotional part of me heal. Finding Stella would mean I had made the right choice for her welfare and my own. What bothered me the most, though, was the knowledge that Mother would have done what I did not have the courage to do. Mother would have protected Stella at any cost. Mother would have given her life freely to see that Stella survived. But what Mother could never have known was a simple camp reality: Giving her life would have been a futile, meaningless act. Had she made such an offer in Birkenau, the Nazis would have gleefully murdered Stella moments before shooting my mother.

I played the scenarios in my mind over and over as the plane droned across Germany on the way to my reunion with Uncle Rahamin in Rome. Such bitter conjectures were a continuous part of the Holocaust aftermath in all of us. What would Mother have done? What could I have said to change a certain situation? Why didn't I fight instead of so innocently permitting Hitler's boot on my neck? Why didn't we all?

The sound of Uncle Rahamin's voice came to me like a wonderful, forgotten song.

"Ah, Laura. You are more beautiful than beauty itself."

I turned, eyes closed, in the direction the song had come from. I could feel people brush past and jostle me in the busy terminal, but I stood my ground. "I am *not* beautiful!" And then I could feel his hands on my shoulders, and I opened my eyes. His were staring straight into mine and were filled with tears.

"You are the most beautiful sight I have ever seen."

Our embrace was desperate, as if we were both trying to absorb a part of us that had been lost. I tried to smell Father's cigarette smoke in his clothing, tried to hear the clatter of the old streets in the sounds of his words, tried to hug Mother's waist as I clutched at him. But there was nothing there. For while the sound of his voice was familiar, there was nothing of the inner confidence and smooth intonation that had always been unique to Uncle Rahamin.

Instead, a broken man held me. He was thin, almost gaunt, and seemed little more than a shell of the Uncle Rahamin I had known. It was obvious that, at some time during his stay in the camps, his spirit had been beaten out of him, or at least he had seen so many horrors that he had forgotten himself. But he had not forgotten me.

"Are you well, Laura?"

"I'm OK," I said, "and you?"

He smiled a little, and I could tell there was so much I didn't know. For while he was genuinely happy to see me, there was a deep sadness to him that was nearly unfathomable. I had seen it before. Uncle Rahamin's eyes betrayed the same kind of inner turmoil I had seen in Benjamin, Sima, and all the others. There were secrets here that couldn't be told, at least not now. I wondered if Uncle saw the same thing in my gaze.

And like everyone else who had survived, we didn't talk about the camps. Instead, I asked about Joseph and Asher, questioned where Uncle lived in Rome and who was taking care of his needs, wondered aloud at how eerie it was to step from one culture to another.

It was warm here, unlike the cold Swedish winter I had just come from. How odd it all was, but I seemed to be continually stepping through cultures and lives. Lives so unique and memorable, yet so unconnected except for my brief passage into and out of each one. At times I had to stop and wonder if the world I was in was real. I felt so lost and disconnected most of the time; lost from the family I had known all my life, disenfranchised from a culture that no longer existed.

But I know I wasn't alone in my pain. The look in Uncle Rahamin's eyes and in those of us survivors told me so. We almost never talked of Rhodes or those who were not among us. Neither did we speak of the past, even, as I now discovered, among family. No one wanted to be reminded of what had happened.

So, too, it seemed that as I settled into a huge survivors' house that had been provided by the Jewish community in Rome, I noticed this strange, lonely depression in many others. Many Italians—normally such happy, vivacious people—seemed to stroll about the streets as if they did not know where to go, did not know what to do. I could see it in them as I saw it in all the others. Huge chunks of their personal lives had been ripped away by the war: Sons and daughters and lovers and friends gone forever. They looked a little stunned, more than a little lost. Like the shell-shocked soldier now home from battle, they struggled to find normalcy again. The trouble was that nothing was as it had been, save the streets and buildings they had occupied in a different world. It seemed at times that no one in Rome was without some kind of deep personal loss. We would nod to each other as we passed in the streets, a silent acknowledgment of the pain and loneliness we shared.

Yet there were differences between these lonely Roman citizens and us survivors from Rhodes. At least the shell-shocked soldier from Rome had a home to return to. We had none. Of the nearly two thousand of us they had shipped away in the boats that day, I was one of 104 who survived. There was no chance of reconstituting a community that had existed for a thousand years and that now had over ninety percent of its population exterminated. To even try would have been an invitation to living with loss beyond words.

Of course, I knew none of this at the time. If I had, I believe to this day I would have died. As it was, I would sometimes wake at night and think I was in that little room at home with Asher. Then, as my senses came to me, I would realize that home had evaporated without a trace—at least for now. What was worse, my memories of it were beginning to fade, just as my parents had turned to shadows.

I have heard the stories about entire communities being wiped out by the Nazis during the war. I have heard of those small hamlets in Europe that simply ceased to exist through the execution of their entire populace. I envy them, for at least in their case, there is no one left without a sense of home.

But there was still a sense of community and helpfulness here, for even as we suffered together, we also worked together to begin to make things better. The Jewish community in Rome went to great lengths to make us comfortable, even though none of us could call the survivors' house our home. They were wonderful to us, kind and considerate of our experiences. They arranged picnics and other social events for us, so that we could at least feel a sense of normalcy. But it wasn't easy. There was always that underlying, unspoken secret that haunted all of us. It had been over a year since I was liberated, and mine still haunted me. Where was Stella?

I had barely been in Rome two weeks when, with Uncle Rahamin's help, I took the train to Bologna to see Joseph and Asher. And while Rome itself seemed a more or less normal city, the countryside revealed the truth of the Italians' suffering. It had been more than a year since the end of hostilities, but I rode past villages that were little more than burned-out shells of their former selves, fields that still bore the pockmarks of countless shells and bombs, farmhouses and barns that could no longer shelter anything. It reminded me of that terrible walk I had taken across Germany.

Still, while the marks of destruction remained, so, too, the resiliency of the people shone like the new grass that grows from a burned-over field. I realized that the rails I rode on could not have remained intact throughout the Allied invasion. They had most certainly been repaired. I could see taking place here and there the construction of new buildings or the repair of those that could be restored. I suppose I was not unlike this whole country, this whole continent, the world itself. There were signs of the horrors we had been through everywhere. Signs that reminded each of us of our individual suffering. But we were recovering, some slowly, some rapidly. We chose to rebuild our farm houses, and we made decisions to look ahead to an uncertain future rather than looking back to a horrific past. It was all part of healing. Whether a world or a country or a village or just Laura Varon, we were beginning to reassemble the bricks of our shattered lives again. As I sat there on the train, I realized why we seldom spoke of the camps. It was only partially the brutality and horror we had seen. It was just as much the fact that as we placed the bricks together again, we all knew that there was no way life would be the same as it had been when we were finished. There was little point in looking back, save to remember the blue-prints of the lives we were working to re-create. Those drawings were made in Rhodes or in a peaceful Rome or in villages before the tanks shattered them. Our focus now had to be on taking the best from before the butchery and building better lives and a better world: A world that broke the barriers our collective traditions had built; lives that excluded the prejudice and bigotry that had created the Holo-caust. After a while, I dozed as the train jostled along, and for once I did not fear a nightmare. For once, I did not feel so alone.

There was a wonderful strangeness about my reunion with Joseph and Asher, a surreal, loving meeting with few words. They were wait-ing for me at the train station in Bologna along with a few other survivors from Rhodes: Albert Hannan, the brother of Pepo, the soc-cer player I had cheered for so long ago; and Diana, Felicia, and Gineta Galante, three sisters who had miraculously survived and found each other. But they all appeared to me as if in a magical vision from the crowded ramp, and I could tell from their eyes that I ap-peared the same. The instant I saw them all, everything and every-one else around me ceased to exist. I could have heard the slightest whisper from them, despite the noise of the station, yet I heard noth-ing. There was not a word as I embraced Asher, not a tear as Joseph put his arms around me and kissed my forehead. There was only a look between us that we shared the most intimate knowledge of experience and a thankful bewilderment that somehow we had sur-vived that experience. It was as if our very souls were all in the same place at the same time, and I believe to this day that they were. There was no need for words, for the majesty of that moment said everything to all of us. Felicia took my hand and I could feel her inside me. Albert put his arm around me, and I could feel his trem-bling pain and joy. For those few moments there on the ramp beside the train, Rhodes existed again, and its power infused us all. It was a moment I shall carry beyond the grave, for God let us see the blueprint as if it had just been drawn.

Joseph, Asher, and I were entranced, for the magic of our moments at the train station seemed to impress on us how wonderfully blessed we were to still have one another. Our words came slowly at first, but they were joyous and positive. We never spoke of the camps, or the fact that Mother and Father weren't there, or that none of us knew about Stella. For the most part, we spoke, instead, of wonderful, real-life trivialities. Joseph talked about the villages he visited nearby to read Hebrew during their Jewish celebrations. Asher spoke of his classes. But there was so much meaning to our seemingly meaningless conversations. We were building life as it should have been. We were each, in our own way, forcing ourselves to live in the present and view the future positively. My days in Bologna would be spent reveling in our trivialities. I stayed in a dormitory-like house that the Jewish community there had established for survivors.

But there were still indignities to endure, still quiet persecutions to make us feel alone. While I was in Bologna, we received a letter from the Greek embassy that extended Greek citizenship to all Rhodes survivors. Rhodes, after all, had been given to Greece after the war, and the letter I received appeared at first to be a kind recognition that we all had a right to return if we so desired. But part of our tradition in Rhodes was the fact that we were all Italian citizens. We had been raised under Italian rule. The Italian government had made many improvements to life on Rhodes while we lived there. We all sent the letters back, stating that we believed ourselves to be Italian citizens and intended to stay that way.

Apparently, the Greek government decided that Italian citizens could not live under Greek rule. A few weeks after sending our responses to the embassy, we received another letter. It stated that since we refused Greek citizenship, we could not come back to Rhodes to live. In fact, if we were even to visit the island, our stay could last no longer than six months.

I believe that, at the time, few of us thought that a return to Rhodes was practical. To do so would have meant being part of a near-invisible minority, living amid constant reminders of a past that could never be resurrected. Nonetheless, the letters we received served as a formal declaration of our extinction as a community, a reminder that, through no fault of our own, we were now homeless.

Not only was it impractical to return because of our decimation at the hands of the Nazis, it was now officially impossible.

In retrospect, this incident was a lesson to me in what we Jews had learned as a result of the war, not because of the incident itself but because of our response to it. In the old days in Rhodes, such an occurrence would have been met with cowering acceptance, as was the case when Governor de Vecchi closed the Collegio Rabbinico. But in Bologna, we survivors were angry and indignant at the Greek government's treatment of us. Many letters were sent that must have burned the eyes of those unfortunate enough to have to read them. Of course, it didn't change anything. But as I watch the reactions of Jews today, I realize that much of it is a result of what we remember from the war. If Israel had existed in the thirties, she likely would have been a pawn among nations. Today, she can be a vicious source of retribution to those who seek her destruction. The reason lies deep in each of her citizens, in each of us who call ourselves Jews. We have learned the price of innocence, ignorance, and cowering acceptance of what befalls us. We exist today because we understand that peace demands vigilance, that the price of peace is the responsibility of those who enjoy it. Six million of us had to die in the most horrific ways so that we should learn the lesson. In Bologna, I realized those of us who survived had learned it well.

My personal storms of emotion had finally eased to long swells and troughs on a quieter sea. There were still reminders of the horror everywhere, but I was becoming far better at knowing how to avert the deep depression they could instigate. Besides, I was feeling much better these days, and my brothers and the other survivors from Rhodes were a constant source of support and security. I found myself looking ahead more than I was looking back. I found I could even deal with a black envelope.

They came occasionally in the mail. They were notices or, in some cases, confirmation of the death of a loved one. I had seen what they could do to some of my friends who had received them in Sweden. I had seen the tears and heard the wails. So when Albert Hannan handed me one, I shuddered. Would I find Stella's name in the letter? I braced myself for a fall into the pit.

But it was not to be. The letter contained notice of the death of Llia Vytautus, the wonderful Lithuanian woman I had met in the hospital in Stockholm. I smiled sadly, touched deeply that she had thought enough of me to make sure I was informed of her passing. I was surprised the letter had found me, since the address I had given her was in Rome.

The strange thing was that I was happy at the news of Llia's death. Not because it wasn't Stella's name in the letter, but because the news did not throw me into a reminiscence of past horrors; it did not bring horrible nightmares that evening; it did not leave me depressed for days. It was another sad but meaningful sign I was getting better emotionally, like the aftermath of my visit to the synagogue when I had learned of Mother's and Father's deaths. I was happy to realize it.

In Rome, Uncle Rahamin was becoming well established in the Jewish community. Despite the back injury that continued to plague him, he had managed to make many friends and acquaintances in the area, particularly among the Rhodes survivors who had taken up residence there. When he felt able to, he would often join them for relaxation and conversation in the cafes about the city.

But on this particular day, Uncle Rahamin had stayed home from a planned meeting with two of his friends at a small cafe near the Coliseum. The two girls had thus come alone to the place, where they sipped cappuccino and chatted throughout the afternoon. Of course, two young women sitting alone quickly attracted the attention of the seemingly countless soldiers who wandered the streets of Rome in their off-duty hours. Within a fairly short time, the girls were engaged in lively, flirtatious conversation with two Italian soldiers.

But the conversation became serious when the soldiers learned that the girls were Jewish survivors from Rhodes.

"You are from Rhodes? The island of Rhodes?"

"Yes. From the city. The Jewish Quarter. The Juderia."

The soldiers looked at each other for a moment, as if they had just discovered a clue to a long-held mystery.

"Tell me. Do you know of a family from Rhodes with the name of Varon?"

The girls quickly became intent listeners. There seemed to be an instantaneous recognition that the soldiers were about to tell them something important.

"Yes. Yes, we both know people from the family Varon. Living here in Rome."

One of the soldiers lit a cigarette while the other, about to speak, leaned forward across the table. "Then I need to tell you about a young girl named Stella. Stella Varon. Do you know of her?"

The girls became excited. Uncle Rahamin had many times mentioned his search for his niece.

"Yes! Yes! We know they are looking for her. Do you know if she is alive?"

The soldier smiled. "She is alive if Italy's food hasn't killed her. We left her in Merano."

"Merano? She is there? Alive?"

The soldier who had lit the cigarette spoke next. "We were patrolling our sector in Germany, west of Auschwitz, and we came upon some rail cars on a siding. They were cattle cars, just sitting there with the doors locked on the outside."

The girls listened intently as the soldier took a drag on his cigarette.

"Well, they were full of skeletons. I mean, we shot away the locks and when we opened the doors, we found the cars were full of people. Most of them were lying down, and the smell in the cars was as foul as you could imagine. There were many dead with those still alive."

"And Stella was there?"

He nodded. "Yes. Yes. This little thing. This little girl was with all these horrible living skeletons. She seemed the smallest of them all, those that were alive." He took another drag. "But you know, when she learned we were from Italy, she started speaking to us in Italian, yelling at us to take her with us. She was screaming in this little hoarse voice that she had to be in Italy. She had to be in Italy. We had to take her with us."

The soldier shrugged. "So we did. We put her in our truck and took her to camp, and we fed her and gave her some decent clothes to wear. After a few days, she sort of became our little mascot. You know, she was such a sweet little girl. I think she reminded all of us of what we had been fighting for all that time. She reminded us of home and of innocence. She reminded us of our daughters."

"Yes, yes. Sweet little Stella," the other soldier chimed in. "She didn't seem to be sick, just terribly thin from lack of food. After a few days, she became much more active, much more alive than before, you know? The food did her so much good."

One of the girls stood up. "I think we have to leave now. We must go to tell Rahamin of this story."

The soldier with the cigarette held up his hand. "Wait, please. Another minute. I think I can tell you right where she is, if she has not moved since we left her. It was over a year ago, but I'll bet she's still there."

"Where?"

"Well, we were ordered to come back to Merano for supplies. Not a long drive. A couple days, you know? And Stella kept insisting she had to meet her family in Italy. Well, we stuffed little Stella in the truck with us and drove together back across the border. We found a convent in Merano where we left her with some Catholic nuns. You should check with the convent there. They probably know where she is, if she's not still there. It's a small city. I don't remember the name, but I'm sure there can't be that many convents in Merano."

And with that, both girls hurriedly left the cafe. The flirtation of moments before was replaced by warm embraces for the two Italians and kisses of thanks. Stella was alive, somewhere in Merano. Uncle Rahamin had to know right away, and the soldiers understood. They were, after all, Italians. They, like we, knew what it was like to wonder about the fates of loved ones.

Asher burst into my room, breathing heavily from running up the stairs. I stood up abruptly at the intrusion. "Asher! What is the matter?"

My brother's face was flushed from the exertion, and his eyes were filled with tears. He spoke haltingly between deep breaths. "She . . . She is alive, Laura. Stella is alive."

I sat back on the bed without saying anything. I looked up at Asher then slowly out the window. I drew a deep breath. "Please, Asher. Leave me now for a little while." My voice came in that whisper that comes before tears. "Please."

I heard the door latch quietly behind me and my brother's confused footsteps fading down the hallway. I began to cry. Long, loud, trembling wails of guilt erased, of uncertainty released. I spoke aloud to God and Marushka and hoped that Laurina heard me. I pummeled the bed with my fists and cursed the Nazi bastards who had done this to us. And through my tears, Father put his arms around me and slowly rocked me back and forth as he did in the warmth of our home. I heard a song and turned my head to see Mother, humming the tune contentedly with a knowing smile of forgiveness. I cried that afternoon until my tears ran dry. I wailed and cursed and spoke to my memories until I no longer had a voice. And I stood then, quietly leaning against the window frame and staring out into the darkness. I had utterly emptied my emotion and my mind and now reconstructed my conscience with just one thought: Stella was alive. I had done the right thing.

I took a long, deep breath and gazed out the window of the train. The sun warmed the side of my face, radiating heat to me as if I was tending flowers in a greenhouse. But I was not uncomfortable, for the air was crisp and cool. I could smell grasses and wildflowers as the train creaked through mountain meadows. I could almost feel the mist from the waterfalls we passed as we inched along the sides of steep alpine valleys. I inhaled it all. Every sight, every smell, every deep breath, of this freedom. Stella was alive, and I at last had room in my heart to take in my surroundings. I felt as light as the down in a pillow. The breaths I took seemed huge, as if my chest could take in the whole world. I was suddenly no longer congested with the remnants of my pneumonia. I was suddenly no longer straining to hold up under the burden of guilt I had placed on myself.

I didn't know it at the time, but Joseph, Asher, Stella, and I were the only brothers and sisters from any family in Rhodes to have survived intact. The odds against us had probably been immense, but we had somehow won this lottery of chance. Mother and Father, of course, had paid the price of our ticket.

The train slowed as we approached Merano. Nestled in the approaches to the high Alps, it appeared to me a place where one could escape the depression that seemed to grip all of Italy these days. Perhaps it was just my buoyant mood, but I was entranced with the beauty of the countryside here. It was more like I imagined Switzerland or Austria looked than the Italy I had known. Here and there, steep-roofed houses peered out from among the conifers that seemed to dwarf them. Where the land was cleared, sheep and goats grazed on sharp hillsides, or the neat rows of the vintners' vines sat like quilted postage stamps on the edges of the forests. It did not seem as if the tanks had run over this place, or at least I did not see any of the burned-out houses or crushed buildings I had become accustomed to. It seemed to me that this place had survived the ravages of the war, more or less intact. Incredibly, so had Stella.

For some reason, few people had disembarked the train that day, so I saw her almost immediately as I stepped from the car. I was dumbstruck at the sight of her. The little, thin, nearly bald girl I had left at the infirmary stood tall and beautiful before me. Her hair, long and jet black, flowed effortlessly to her shoulders. Her eyes, edged with the dark pall of hunger in the camps, now glistened at me, showing both the innocence of her youth and the mystery of budding womanhood. I just stood there, holding my bag and feeling my throat tighten with my oncoming tears. Stella had not only survived, but physically, at least, she had moved past the horror. To me, she could have stood beside any starlet from any motion picture. I just stood there, feeling rivers of tears flow down my cheeks. She walked up to me, never once diverting her gaze from my eyes. I felt her take my hand, and I knew instantly that the task Mother had given me was, at last, completed. Her composure astounded me, coursed through me, let me know instinctively she was no longer the child I had to care for. Yet, at that instant, those glistening eyes overflowed. We embraced in quiet sobs there beside the train, shedding our tears for the joy of reunion and for those we knew we would never see again.

"Stella. I . . . I." I could barely speak her name, let alone utter a coherent thought. She put her hand against the back of my neck and whispered in my ear.

"I know, sister. They told me everything. I know about the selection, everything. You saved me, Laura. I love you."

I blinked through the tears, and my lips quivered as I whispered back to her. "No, Stella. I took a chance with your life, a horrible choice between uncertainties. God saved your life, Stella, not me. But in saving yours, He saved mine, too. I love you, sister. I wish Mother was here to see us."

Stella now draped her arm across my shoulders, and we began to walk away slowly. "She is, Laura. She is."

As in Rome and in many other Italian cities, Jewish communities in Northern Italy had sponsored and taken care of many Holocaust survivors. Though there were few Jews in Merano, Stella had been placed in the Institute Miravelle, a school and boarding house run by the Catholic archdiocese. It was a beautiful place, and Stella had generously been provided a room to herself. It seemed that if nothing else, everyone in Italy knew of what we survivors had endured and, regardless of their economic means, made special efforts to give us extra care and concern. In the institute, it quickly became apparent to me that even though Stella had been there for some time, she was

still treated as a most special student. Though I met no other survivors there, there were many girls at the school who had obviously
come from poor families, who had been orphaned during the war, or
who had otherwise suffered and been victimized by the Nazi occupation of Italy. At the same time, some of the girls I met were from
rather well-to-do backgrounds and were attending the institute for
its quality of education. Yet, for all the apparent diversity of the
student population, there seemed to be none of the castes so often
apparent in private schools. All the girls seemed to get along together,
and most appeared content with the treatment they received. But
Stella was special. Whether because she was a survivor, or because
until now she was thought to have no family, or simply because she
was a lone Jew in a Catholic school, everyone appeared to treat her
with special respect. It warmed my heart to see that she had been
so well cared for.

Of course, I was the first family member she had seen, and Stella
was full of questions. She had tried, through her Jewish sponsors, to
locate us, but had had no success until that chance meeting in Rome
had prompted a message from Uncle Rahamin. I tried to give her all
the details I knew; I tried to fill in a void that spanned nearly two
years.

Like most conversations among survivors, we talked very little
about the camps. I told her only that Uncle Rahamin had been
beaten by the Nazis in Buchenwald and still had days when he had
trouble walking without severe discomfort. I also told her he had
made many friends in Rome and was beginning to find success in
business. I thought he might stay there permanently, unless Uncle
Nissim convinced him to go to the Belgian Congo.

As for Joseph and Asher, I told Stella about our meeting in Bologna
and how much Joseph's expertise in Hebrew was appreciated in the
local Jewish communities. I told her my worries about Asher. Of all
of us, he seemed the most still troubled about what happened. I
didn't know what his Holocaust secrets were, for he refused ada-
mantly to say anything at all about the camps. And I didn't press the
issue, I said, for he seemed to withdraw instantly into himself if the
subject was even broached. Still, on a day-to-day basis, at least, Asher
was as vibrant and alive as any young man his age. It was just that
there was a secret in him, a secret that he, like I had, struggled to
forget.

By evening, our conversation had turned to lighter matters. Stella talked to me about her studies and the warm relationships she enjoyed with many of the other students and staff.

"... and my best friend on the staff is Luigia, our cook."

I giggled. "Is that how you look so good, Stella? Making friends with the cook?"

My sister smiled back at me with a warmth I hadn't sensed since Rhodes. "Maybe."

There was the sudden sound of a bell that startled me. Stella smiled a little nervously. "It's nothing, sister. The dinner bell." She stood up. "Come, you can meet Luigia." As my sister stood, she reached to touch my arm. "I'll bet she can fatten you up, too, Laura." I laughed again, reveling in the warmth of our togetherness.

Luigia was a short, rotund woman who seemed to be everywhere at once in the dining hall. She was what you would think of as a classic Italian mother, working constantly, talking passionately, and smiling a smile that only mothers know how. She was probably 40 or so and had salt-and-pepper hair pulled straight back from that round, happy face. She seemed to dote on everyone in the room, especially on Stella. I immediately took to her, as I'm sure every girl in the school had at one time or another.

"You are Stella's sister?"

"I am," I said. I put out my hand. "My name is . . ."

"Laura." She smiled as she picked up our dinner plates. "Laurrra." Luigia rolled the sound off her lips. "Such a beautiful name. You are blessed to have such a name, Laura. Blessed. I hope we can talk some, and soon, yes?"

I smiled. Stella grinned at me from her seat across the table, nodding. "Yes. Me too."

That same bell I had heard for dinner awoke me the next morning. Stella was already pulling her clothes on as the bell rang, and I noticed that same nervous smile I had seen the night before. "Classes," she said. "I have to go to class." I rolled back over as the bell stopped ringing, but I sensed there was something more to this than Stella was telling me. But for now at least, it didn't matter. "Six o'clock," I yawned. "Too early." Within moments, I was back asleep.

The next morning was the same. I was awakened by the bell and turned to find Stella hurriedly putting her clothes on. But this time instead of going back to sleep, I waited until Stella had gone. Then I got dressed and went to the dining hall to talk with Luigia.

We sat across a big table from each other in the kitchen. Our conversation was pleasant and cheerful, but during its course, I asked the question that was nagging at me.

"Tell me. Does everyone go to mass here in the mornings?"

"Of course. At the first bell. Then religion class, then breakfast."

"So everyone is in religion class now?"

"Yes. Yes. Then I have to serve breakfast."

I wasn't enraged by the fact that Stella was going to mass and religious school, because I understood that the Institute Miravelle was a place of discipline, and that was part of what made it such a good school. But at the same time, I wondered how much choice Stella had had. If she was attending Catholic services here as an observer, that was one thing. If she had somehow been coerced into these activities, that was quite another. Unfortunately, I suspected the latter, due mainly to my sister's nervous behavior and deception when I asked her about the bell.

The few Jewish families that had sponsored Stella had obviously placed her here because they assumed no harm or deception would come to one who had already endured such hardship. But the institute ran on conformity, and I guessed that Stella had been made to conform with everyone else. While I was sure that no one meant Stella any real harm, it was apparent that the religious zeal or desire for conformity by the staff had overcome their respect for Stella's Jewish heritage. Perhaps she acquiesced because of her fears from past persecution. Perhaps she was attending mass and religion classes because she was grateful to be alive and so well cared for. Regardless of Stella's motivation, I resolved that it was my place as her sister to stand up for her because I could; I believed that what she was enduring wasn't necessary any more. She now had her family back and no longer had to think of herself as alone in a world that still harbored such subtle persecution. I was not mad at the staff, but I was determined to resolve the issue.

The next morning the bell rang as usual, and Stella arose quickly to put on her clothes.

"You don't have to go to mass, Stella."

My sister looked at me in alarm, realizing I knew she was not going to classes.

"It's all right, Stella. It's all right to say no. You aren't in the camps anymore. You can stay here in bed and go to your regular classes after breakfast. Nothing will happen to you."

Tears quickly filled her eyes. "I . . . I have to go, Laura. I have to go. They will kick me out if I do not go to mass."

I sat up in bed. "Stella. Listen to me. If going to mass is a condition of your being in this school, then you shouldn't be here, no matter how nice it is. Remember where you came from and what you were raised to believe. You should not be forced to go to mass or religion class. You do not have to go."

Stella continued putting on her clothes. She was shaking. "I have to go, Laura. No. I have to go."

I threw back the covers in disgust and in an instant, stood inches from my sister's face. "You listen to me, Stella. If you go to mass today you are going to go through that window. I will personally throw you through it, and after you are on the ground, if you are still alive, *then* you can go to mass!"

My face was red with anger. Stella stood staring in my eyes for another second or two. Without saying a word, she removed her clothes and got back in bed.

"I will take care of this, Stella. You do not have to go to mass."

The door to the Monsignor's office swung open with a quiet creak. After some discussion with both the housekeeper and the priest who served as the Monsignor's secretary, I had been permitted this discussion. Monsignor Mazzell stood near his desk and motioned me to a seat nearby. He was a tall, intimidating figure. Though his desk separated us, he appeared to glower at me from behind his glasses. He stood stiffly, and his robes seemed to enhance his serious demeanor.

"Stella was not at mass this morning."

I looked squarely into his eyes. "Monsignor Mazzell, with all respect, I have come to tell you that my sister is not going to change her religion. We are Jewish and we will die Jewish."

The Monsignor looked away for a moment then returned my gaze. "You know, Miss Varon, we believe that those who die without being baptized will go to hell."

I could feel my anger sear my consciousness, but I did not get up from my chair. I did not scream at him. I merely stared straight into his eyes. "Don Mazzell, you have every right to believe what you believe. But you have no right to attempt to make my sister have those same beliefs by coercion."

"Coercion?" His voice raised, just a little.

"Yes, coercion. You have taken advantage of Stella's sensitivities, and in doing so, you blaspheme what you believe. You blaspheme God. You blaspheme the memory of my parents." I could feel my voice quiver a little, but I quickly found the strength to focus my anger.

"My mother and father died because they were Jewish. I have seen babies ripped apart before my eyes. I am one of only a hundred or so still alive out of a community of two thousand Jews." I got up from my seat and walked around the desk to face him. My eyes were dark with a quiet rage.

"Don Mazzell, I have seen your hell. I have seen what the man-made hypocrite you call God allowed to happen to Jews and gypsies and Catholics and anyone else His bigotry deemed unfit for existence. I have seen your hell, Monsignor, and I have survived it to bring people like you a message. God did not create the hell you talk about. You did."

The Monsignor did not say anything. He only blinked at my words.

"As for Stella and me, we will honor the memory of our people. We will remain what we are, what our parents were, what our grandparents taught us to be. Stella will not be coming to mass tomorrow, Monsignor, nor any mass on any day." I began to turn away, then I turned back to him again. My voice was calm, but I nearly spit the words at him.

"I do not expect a decision on this matter from you, Don Mazzell. I demand your respect."

The office door clicked shut quietly behind me. I nodded politely to the priest in the reception area and acknowledged the housekeeper who now worked quietly in the hall.

I could hear my footsteps echoing down the corridor. Slowly, they became faster and faster as I strode away from the Monsignor's offices. By the time I reached the kitchen, I was running.

Apparently, word of my discussion, or at least the reason for my discussion, had traveled fast. I could tell that Luigia knew from the look on her face. She said absolutely nothing. She simply sat me down at that big table in the kitchen, poured me a glass of warm milk, and triggered my tears with a gentle hand on my shoulder.

Stella never again went to morning mass. When she came back from school that day, I told her that she would not have to go anymore. The Monsignor had said nothing about whether Stella would be permitted to stay in the school or not, but I really knew he had little choice in the matter. To expel Stella would have been to publicize the fact that her Jewish faith was not respected in the school. And regardless of the feelings of the Catholic community about religious instruction, such publication would have been political suicide for the Monsignor. The world outside his office was changing; it had been forced to change because of the war. People were trying desperately to help one another, to somehow rebuild meaning into their lives, and their humanitarianism overrode religious boundaries. I'm not saying that Italy in 1947 had suddenly become an egalitarian utopia; the Monsignor's behavior had certainly demonstrated otherwise. But there was genuine concern for the plight of others everywhere. After Mussolini, Hitler, and the generals who carried out their whims, authoritarian acts were not something the populace would have taken lightly.

And so it was that Stella and I would stay. She continued to attend classes, and I continued to heal. Little by little I was getting stronger, and the people and countryside around Merano did much to help. As I had done in Stockholm, I found myself wandering through the parks and public places around the town, and the beauty of this place never did cease to entrance me. Whether my physical healing drove my emotional recovery or the reverse I don't know, but I was slowly beginning to feel sensations I had not known since Rhodes. I was carefree here in Merano, and I had the blessed freedom to make choices strictly for myself. I embraced it, sucked it in like those deep breaths I had taken on the train, but freedom was still something I was getting used to. I seemed to be so involved and needing the sensation of freedom itself that I spent little time discerning whether the decisions I made were the right ones.

Nonetheless, life had become wonderful and warm here in the cool mountain air. The people at the institute were caring, conscientious people who did their best to make Stella and me comfortable. The Jewish families who sponsored us often invited us to dinner, to outings, or to accompany them to synagogue. The townspeople in Merano always seemed to smile.

But our short, magical life in Merano was to change significantly. After I had been there about two months, Uncle Nissim sent word that Stella would travel to Rome to meet Uncle Rahamin, and they were both going to meet him in the Belgian Congo. I was to remain in Merano alone to continue my recuperation. Once again, I would be alone.

There was, of course, a difference between being alone and free and being alone without hope. Though I missed Stella terribly after she left, I still had opportunities to travel to Bologna to visit Joseph and Asher, and I had made several friends with the students and staff at the institute. We spent many wonderful days together in Merano, and I found ways to, at least temporarily, erase my loneliness by helping in the day-to-day chores of the institute staff. As always, Luigia was like a mother to me.

My loneliness and free time these days seemed to put me in a contemplative mood. What was I to do with the rest of my life? Why had my innocence, both figuratively and literally, been stripped away so brutally? How could I reconcile what had happened with what was expected of me as a normal citizen in a civilized community? I harbored so much anger and resentment toward the German people and anyone else that I felt remotely was responsible for the Holocaust. I realized I had to find a way to channel my anger positively, for the alternative was to sink to the same depths of brutality that those who had persecuted me possessed. Whether justified or not, I knew how much I could hurt people by acting out my aggressive fantasies, particularly against anyone who spoke the German language. I needed to find a way to stifle my instincts for revenge, yet satisfy that thirst at the same time. I thought that perhaps helping others in some meaningful way would be the answer. How fortunate I was to have the time to be able to stand back and see it.

There is no question in my mind that God was with me while I was in Merano. He gave me the strength to stand up to the Monsignor; He gave me the peaceful world of Northern Italy in which to heal; He found ways to make me smile again, despite my occasional bouts with sickness. I remembered how I had felt that He owed me when I first visited the synagogue in Stockholm. In Merano, it was as if God had heard me. It seemed that He was somehow trying to make up for those months in the camps when He had forsaken all of us. Though we both knew He never could, there were moments in Merano when I knew He stood at my shoulder.

The headmaster at the institute had noticed how depressed I seemed to be and had arranged an introduction with two doctors who worked in a nearby veterans hospital. They came the short distance to the institute specifically to talk with me and to see if I would be interested in volunteering as an assistant at the hospital. Such coincidences, whether arranged or not, seemed to be happening to me constantly. No sooner had I been thinking about helping others as a means to helping myself than the opportunity presented itself. Of course I would volunteer. Perhaps I could even learn something about nursing.

Like the institute, the doctors and nurses at the hospital were sincere, loving caregivers. They tended their patients with the same sort of intense compassion I had received in Stockholm. Their patients were almost exclusively Italian war veterans who were either still recovering from wounds inflicted in battle or who were suffering from chronic disease.

Everyone knew I was a survivor, and the doctors and nurses felt that by talking with some of the patients, I could lend a unique understanding and compassion for their plight. I had, after all, seen at least as much disease, brutality, and hardship as any of them, and I knew what it was like to lie in a hospital bed for days on end. So I found myself spending the last hour or so of my shift simply wandering around among the patients, making friends and sharing feelings.

Of course, God was at my shoulder, and I'm sure He knew that those conversations were doing as much for me as I was able to do for the patients. After all, he gave me Michele.

He was a young Italian of about 25 who had been at the hospital ever since the war ended. He suffered from tuberculosis, and by the time I met him, he was terribly thin and plagued by a cough that never seemed to stop. When I first began visiting his bedside, he reminded me of so many I had seen in the camps. His eyes were dark and set deep in gray-black sockets, and I remembered that first time I had looked in a mirror. His hair was cropped short and thin, and I remembered the way Jaco and Salvo looked that day before the truck took them away forever. And he was so gaunt from the ravages of his disease.

But unlike so many who stood before me with bodies ravaged by disease and malnutrition, Michele's mind was clear and seemingly unhampered by his malady. He suffered through his miseries stoically and always seemed to have the strength for a joke to make me laugh. Perhaps it was that wonderful wit that made me find my way to his bedside more frequently than to the others. Perhaps it was that I could see the handsome young man he had been before his disease ravaged him. Regardless, I found myself strangely attracted to this man I barely knew, but I deluded myself into believing my attraction was the result of his need for someone to talk to. I realized far too late that it was based on my need for him.

We talked about everything imaginable, Michele and I, about everything from his family and experiences in the war to many of my horrors in the camps. For some reason, he was unique in that respect. I could talk with Michele without fear. He would simply touch my hand as the quiet tears came to my eyes, and he gave me the strength to relive things I could not relive. He seemed to know so well my emotional limits, as if through that thin hand on mine, a current of intimate knowledge passed between us. Without so much as a pause, and without the pity I despised, Michele would redirect our conversation just as I was about to cry out from a memory I had suppressed. We would suddenly be talking about dreams, about the future, when seconds before I was watching Mother disappear forever.

"Laura, when I am out of here and really better, I want to marry you."

I stared into Michele's dark eyes, and I knew this was not a ploy to pull me away from my tears. His seriousness struck me, made me gasp without any visible sign of surprise. It was an honest proposal, and I realized our attraction ran far deeper than shared conversation, shared emotions of the past and present. A future stared up at me from that bed in the hospital. A future I could grasp with a simple smile through the tear that dribbled down my cheek.

I wiped it away with the back of my hand. The question had caught me totally off-guard, and I responded in the only way I knew I could without giving a direct answer. I needed time to think about this, but I couldn't tell him why.

"You know, Michele, I've been told that those of us who have not been baptized will go to hell."

Michele laughed a little, and it made him cough. "That's garbage, Laura. Garbage. Don't pay any attention to those people." He coughed again. "Besides, I would gladly go to hell if you were there with me."

We both laughed, but we both knew the seriousness of the moment. I stood up from beside him and put on my coat. "I have to go, Michele."

He reached for my hand and gave it a little squeeze. He smiled, but that seriousness in his eyes told me his question was real. I walked quietly past the end of his bed and then turned again to him. "I'll think on it, Michele. I will."

I was not prepared for this. I was not prepared for commitment. Michele's proposal flattered me and depressed me at the same time. I so much needed, I believed, to give to others, yet I was unready to give that much to another person. I realized just how far away I was from truly being able to give emotional sustenance to others. Sure, I could talk and I could share experiences. I could cry with them and I could hold their hands. But I was taking more from the experience than I was able to give. I was still healing those deep wounds, still revealing those deep secrets. Until I had finished, I could not share myself totally.

I put it out of my mind. I avoided answering Michele's question either to him or to myself. For two days I occupied myself helping Luigia in the kitchen, or took chatty, meaningless walks with my friends. I avoided Michele's bed the next day when I went to work at the hospital. But I knew I owed this gentle man an answer, and I knew what that answer must be. Though I did not have to work until the next night, I walked through the evening streets to see Michele.

I pushed open the double doors to the ward where he stayed. I walked quickly between the rows of the sick and pulled back the curtain that surrounded his bed. It was empty. Confused, I went to the next bed and gently pulled the curtains there. A gray-haired man slept quietly with his back to me. I walked back down the ward, through the double doors, to the nursing station.

"Where is Michele? Was he moved?"

The nurse at the station paused from her paperwork to look across the desk at me. "Laura, Michele died two nights ago. He died in peace, Laura."

I turned and walked quickly away without saying a word. I strode out of the hospital as rapidly as I had come in, and I was out of breath by the time I reached my room at the institute. Michele had died. He was gone, and I had not been there to give him an answer. I had not been there to make his last moments easier. I threw myself on the bed in tears and cried for him. Michele had died. Not in peace, no, for he had never received my answer. Then, again, perhaps he knew.

Uncle Rahamin's time in the Belgian Congo had not been easy. Within weeks of arriving there, his back injuries became progressively worse, and his prior improvements seemed to vaporize in the humidity and heat of the African climate. The doctors there told him he should return to Italy immediately, where the climate, and particularly the care he would receive, was far better for his condition. With Uncle Nissim's help, arrangements were made for his return and for his stay in Cortina d'Ampezzo, a sanitorium near Merano that specialized in treatments of the type he needed.

At about the same time, I had decided to become a nurse. I suppose I felt that after all I had been through, there was little suffering of others that I couldn't deal with, and there was very much I could do for those who were sick or infirm. Besides, I thought, helping others heal would help me heal. Helping others might somehow make up for all the people in the camps I was never able to help. Though Uncle Nissim was very concerned about my decision, he assented to my enrollment in a two-year nursing program. While he worried about my working with the sick after all I had been through personally, at least the school was not far from the institute. I would not have trouble adjusting to another new city. Though I would have to move into the new school, I would still have my friends from the institute and my brothers and my uncle to visit.

So it was that I began my schooling in nursing. The school was operated by Catholics, as it seemed most institutions were in this part of Italy. Though the religious aspects of the institute were absent here, we still worked within a very disciplined schedule. We woke to bells, went to classes by bells, ate by bells, and slept by bells. But I was used to that, for after all the time in the institute, I understood that it was just the Church's way of doing things. And the instructors were wonderful. I remember the Italian doctor who led most of our classes. He was a rotund, jovial man with a unique ability to make us laugh at what was normally depressing, yet he made us learn what was most important. He made nursing a fascinating subject. He made each of us feel as if we were being taught individually, and I found myself excited to attend his classes each day. Between our classes and required apprenticeship in the hospital, those days passed rapidly.

For most of us, I think life had at last begun to take on some form of consistency, of normalcy. I attended my classes and found many new friends in the school. Uncle Rahamin settled in to recuperate from his injuries. Asher worked and attended a school of his own. And Joseph found love.

Her name was Miriam, a petite, blonde young woman from the

Jewish Quarter of Rome. Though Uncle Rahamin balked at their plans to marry, Joseph knew his heart, and it seemed that no amount of argument or discussion would dissuade him. He married Miriam in a very private ceremony in Rome. Though my classes prevented me from attending, I was most happy for my brother and the new life he was creating for himself. For Joseph especially, love gave him the opportunity to forget what he could of the past.

At the same time, Stella was miserable in the Belgian Congo, and though Uncle Nissim tried his best to provide a good environment for her, she had become more despondent as time passed. She missed her friends at the institute horribly and found little in the African countryside to her liking

It seemed to me that Uncle Nissim was the most understanding man in the world. Living thousands of miles from most of us, he had been the single person not only to find us, but to care for us so much after the terror of what we had been through. It was not simply good fortune that had bestowed on him a successful business and fortune in the Belgian Congo. It was the fact that he was a unique man. Uncle Nissim was the kind of person who never forgot his friends, particularly his family. If someone needed help, they turned to him first, and he nearly always found a way to assist. As such, he was very well liked in the business communities of both Belgium and the Belgian Congo, which contributed significantly to his success. Were it not for that, it would have been much more difficult for him to help my brothers, Uncle Rahamin, and me, but I believe he would have found a way regardless of his circumstances. He was that kind of person.

As for Stella, Uncle Nissim realized after a time that the Belgian Congo was not the place for her. After long thought and communication with family members, he decided to send Stella to Seattle, in the United States. There was a rather large Rhodes community there, and family relatives had quickly agreed to provide room and board for her. And since he had not seen Joseph, Asher, or me, he decided to bring Stella to Rome himself before taking an extended vacation in the United States.

I don't remember much about the circumstances of our reunion, for I was so embroiled in the emotions of it that all else seemed to pale. I cried long, loud tears with this man who had done so much to bring us back together. I told him how much his support had meant to me, and I thanked him repeatedly for finding me in Sweden. But Uncle Nissim just held me close to him, smiling through his tears.

"You do not need to thank me, Laura. Seeing you well and alive is more than thanks enough." He put his arm around me and spoke to me as he had so many times, so long ago it seemed, in Rhodes. "You know, I have many friends in the Congo, many good people who help me and who I try to help. But Laura, I have no one who means as much to me as you and your brothers." He looked up a moment. "I would have done anything to find you and Uncle Rahamin and anyone else from the family who might have survived. There were many times during the war, Laura, when I wasn't sure I would have anyone after it ended. I felt so remote, so far away from being able to do anything."

Uncle Nissim began laughing suddenly. "But now, now Laura, I have all of your troubles to deal with. My brother is full of pain. Stella dislikes the Congo. You were sick and sick again." He looked at me with the warmest smile I had ever seen, his brown eyes framed by a face that represented everything we had ever been. "And it's so wonderful, Laura! It is so wonderful to feel something and to be able to do things for those you love! You do not need to thank me, Laura. You have thanked me simply by being alive."

It had been almost two years since I had seen Stella, and I was almost dumbfounded by her beauty. What had begun in Italy had been perfected in the Congo. She had grown into a beautiful woman, and I wondered to myself how long it would be before she would be happily married and raising a family of her own.

Of course, Stella and Uncle Nissim and I had many long conversations during their short stay, and I had the opportunity to accompany them when they went to see Uncle Rahamin and my brothers. And while Uncle Nissim was taking Stella with him to the United States, he had previously made arrangements for Asher and Joseph to go to the Belgian Congo. The reasons were simple: There was a large Jewish community there, and many of its people were originally from Rhodes. The economy in the Congo was booming, and there were many opportunities for people like my brothers to start or work in successful businesses. And most of all, there was Uncle Nissim. Like almost everyone, he had lost nearly all of his immediate family in the camps. He wanted us all to be together if possible or at least to be within reach of one another. Stella's situation notwithstanding, I suppose that if there was a reward for all that Uncle Nissim had done for us, it was that he might be able to be close to us, might be able to see us and care for us, in the Congo. While we never talked about the fact directly, it was something I believe we all understood. For the man who had done so much, it was a price we were all prepared to pay, regardless of whether or not we really wanted to live in Africa. Besides, the opportunities there were every bit as real as Uncle Nissim had described. As such, Joseph and his wife, along with Asher, left for the Congo soon after Uncle Nissim left Italy for the United States. By the time Uncle had returned to the Congo, both Joseph and Asher were working in the import business in different parts of the country.

Uncle Rahamin, of course, became the only close relative I had left in Italy. The poor man had not fared well in the Congo and was now forced to stay in bed almost constantly. I felt so sorry for him, but despite his misery, I also began to see the old Uncle Rahamin reappearing. Though he was constrained, he had regained that twinkling smile for me, and it was obvious that his outlook had changed much for the better. He spoke of the future, of getting out of this place and back on his feet. He was assuming responsibility again, for more than just himself. He seemed to be taking on the role of a father to those of us within his reach, as he had done when he advised Joseph regarding his marriage.

Before leaving, Uncle Nissim had asked me if I wanted to travel with him in the United States. I'm sure he would have welcomed the companionship, and I was tempted to be able to see far-away places and relatives I had never met. But I was happy in Merano. I had found contentment in helping the sick and much happiness in my friends and acquaintances around the community. I wanted to finish nursing school and then, I told him, I would decide what I wanted to do and where I wanted my future to be. While he was still concerned about my health and my work in the hospital, Uncle Nissim consented to my request to stay. I think he understood the contentment in my eyes. Still, I knew his desire was to have me live in the Congo with my brothers and him. I knew I owed him that, and I could only delay the inevitable for so long.

8.

DIRECTION

THE WATERS of the Congo River are black. You can look into them, and it is as if your reflection is swallowed whole by the darkness, as if your stare will never be returned. To travel the Congo, you must become a part of its black, insistent purpose. You must consent to whatever mysteries it might impose. You must try to accept the vacant stares that come at you from its shores and try not to scream when the crocodiles gaze into your eyes from those black waters.

But the Congo is alive in its darkness. With a strength of purpose greater than the Nile, the Congo carries black life through the heart of Africa. It carves an arc across the equator and saps the rainforests of their moisture. It provides an avenue for commerce more than a thousand miles long, yet it frustrates the seafarer with massive cataracts before it reaches the ocean. Most rivers seem to come from some ignominious little stream or pool high in their headlands. The Congo seems to come from everywhere in a massive push to rid the land of its humidity and daily downpours that equal as much as seven feet of rain a year.

I had boarded the steamer in Leopoldville and now looked back on the city from the middle of this wide, black river.

The boat seemed as broad as it was long. Like all the passenger steamers I had seen during my occasional visits to the river, it was something more than a hundred feet long, with multiple decks seemingly crammed to the gunwales. Flat-bottomed with a shallow draft to navigate right up to the shorelines, the vessel now chugged its way against the main current of the river, carrying me lazily toward unknown adventures. Leopoldville didn't fade away to nothingness

as Rhodes had. It simply disappeared behind the islands of the Stanley Pool, its clatter replaced by the chatter of the birds along the
river, its whistles and horns replaced by the screeches of monkeys
and the roars of the animals at night.

I sat near the stern for several hours that first day. Leaning with
my elbows atop the short railing, head in hands, I could peer into
that black water or gaze out as the city disappeared behind us. There
would be little to do, I thought, but enjoy the ride for the next eight
days. There was little to do but feel the slight coolness the river
provided, enjoy the sights along the way, and reflect.

For the last six months since arriving in the Congo, I had been
living aimlessly in Leopoldville with Uncle Nissim. I suppose I had
been something of a bitch to the poor man, for I resented the perceived control he exercised over me in bringing me here. I resented
the heat and the way I seemed to sweat constantly. I resented the
hundred black faces I would see each day compared to the one or
two white faces. I had already suffered the consequences of being a
part of a religious minority. Now I had become part of a racial one,
and it made me uneasy. Perhaps it had all been my adaptation to
new surroundings, but my treatment of Uncle Nissim and, for that
matter, my brothers had been despicable.

Frustrated with my petulance, Uncle Nissim had finally insisted
that I go to visit my brothers. He had sat me down at the kitchen
table, treating me like the child I had become emotionally.

"Laura, it is time you went to visit your brothers, yes?"

"No. Why? Why should I want to go?" I sat at the table, arms
crossed, gazing haughtily at the floor.

Uncle Nissim banged his fist on the table, angrily obtaining my
attention. "Because you have not seen them since Italy, Laura! It
has been nearly a year!" He leaned forward, bringing his eyes to
within inches of mine.

"Now, Laura, I will give you a choice. Do you want to fly or take
the river? Which will it be? Answer me now."

My attitude changed in an instant. Though seeing my brothers
had been something Uncle Nissim had always been more than willing to pay for, I had steadfastly refused his invitations until now. I
had not thought of the river. I had only dreaded another airplane
flight full of bumps in the air, full of my silly fear.

"The river? I can go on the river?"

"Of course, Laura. Is that what you will do?"

I regained a small bit of my petulance. "If you insist, Uncle. If you insist."

I could see some crocodiles basking along a small strip of beach that appeared among the trees overhanging the bank. Jaws agape in the heat, they seemed to be slow, cumbersome creatures. From my perspective, they looked incapable of killing, of even moving quickly enough to capture prey.

Poor Uncle Nissim. The man had done everything for me, and I knew he would still help me in any way he could. Why was I so angry to be with him? I remembered a conversation we had had a couple months after I had arrived in Leopoldville.

"So if you are so miserable here, Laura, where do you want to go? What do you want to do with your life?"

Several of my friends from nursing school had told me they were going to Australia after graduation. "I think I want to go to Australia, Uncle."

"Australia?" Uncle looked perplexed. "Why there? What's there that isn't here?"

"My friends," I shrugged. "You know, I think I want to do something good for people, like I was doing in Merano. I think I need to pay back the Red Cross for all they did for me, you know?"

"But Australia, Laura? You need to go there?" Uncle held out his hands plaintively. "There is a Red Cross here, Laura. And God knows there's plenty of disease to cure."

"Still, Uncle, I think I might like Australia. I've never been there, you know?"

Uncle Nissim turned away from me, lighting a cigarette. "Laura, you haven't been here yet! You haven't seen anything or been anywhere past a few blocks down the street! And your family is here."

I didn't say anything. I just sat staring past him, casually avoiding his eyes and an answer. I knew that would bother him.

"Oh, OK, Laura. You want to go to Australia? OK, I'll arrange for it."

I still didn't say anything, nor did he. He simply walked out of the room.

I stared down at that black water slipping past the riverboat. Poor Uncle Nissim. Within a few days of our talk he had produced both airline tickets and a visa for Australia. I remembered staring numbly at them, turning the visa over in my hand. "I don't want to go after all, Uncle."

"What!?"

"I'm sorry. I didn't think you were serious. I, . . . I don't want to go to Australia."

I suppose that episode was rather typical of the way I'd treated him. Yet this man who had done so much for me still treated me with kindness and respect. It seemed, in fact, that the more abuse I heaped on him the kinder he became. He gave me beautiful jewelry. He personally introduced me to a wealthy friend who had expressed an interest in me and who I subsequently spurned, probably because Uncle Nissim had had something to do with it. He had even arranged a job for me in the local Red Cross clinic, which I thought I would love. The country, after all, was riddled with syphilis, tuberculosis, yellow fever, sleeping sickness, malaria, and a host of other diseases. My first week at the clinic I sat at a small desk and checked patients in. My second week, I took blood from many of the same patients. By the third week, I was back in Uncle's living room, wondering what I should do and where I should turn next.

What was wrong with me? Why did I so dislike this place? Why did I take such pleasure in making Uncle Nissim's life a misery?

Nothing seemed to matter here, and nothing seemed to interest me. I had tasted freedom in Italy, sucked it in like that cool mountain air. But here I took advantage of freedom. The control Uncle Nissim exercised—if it could be called that—was certainly no worse than the teachers and doctors in Merano had had over me. I closed my eyes. Why did I resent him so? Why was I so bored in this clean, beautiful city called Leopoldville? Most of all, why was I so directionless?

I went to my cabin after taking supper in the dining room. I fell asleep to the quiet hissing of the steamer, my questions still unanswered in the darkness of my room within the deep, black waters of the Congo River.

It seemed that, at every bend in the river, we stopped at a village or small town. We would sometimes stop five or six times in a day's travel, taking on cargo in one village only to drop off passengers just across the river in another. But each place we stopped had its own personality, its own unique people and setting. Many times we were permitted to get off the steamer for a half-hour or so while cargo was loaded. In other places, we could only watch the activities on the shoreline or dock from aboard. I'd never noticed the differences among the black people in Leopoldville, but I saw it clearly in those villages. Each stop seemed to represent a different culture, a different set of customs, a different set of colors. There was so much more diversity here than I had realized. From Maluku to Langa-Langa to Lidji, every thatched village of huts or group of houses represented a different lifestyle and, indeed, a different history. There were tribes here that had existed hundreds, even thousands, of years before our time. Though a few tribes had been "modernized," most still lived in those small groups of huts along the shoreline.

I think my entrancement with the Congo came as we turned into the Kasai River, a broad Congo tributary that led to my destination of Port-Franqui. It seemed to pierce the jungle eastward, seemed to be leading me away from any sense of civilization. But I wasn't afraid, except perhaps of the crocodiles and watersnakes that I feared could somehow creep into my cabin. I was too astounded to be afraid. Along the Kasai, a million birds of a thousand colors swooped and dipped and waded along the water's edge. Along the Kasai, the jungle bloomed, brilliant splotches of color set amid the deep green of the jungle that tried to strangle the river. Sometimes you could see animals at the bank, too. Zebra and monkeys and an occasional group of hippos. At night, the jungle would drown out the steamer's engine, burst through the walls of my cabin with the slowly passing sounds of the nocturnal hunt, the obstreperous roar of the predator, and the eerie wails of the prey. Between our village stops on the Kasai, my boredom with life in the Congo ceased forever. I sat staring in awe at what I saw in Nature those days. I sat in wonder at the variety of humankind I observed in the villages. For me, the Congo burst forth from her heat and rain. I realized they only veiled an amazing part of the world from the eyes of the unknowing.

I found myself less fearful of the crocodiles, less unsure of my place in this world. I slowly began to answer those questions that had plagued me as we crossed the Stanley Pool. "I'm sorry, Uncle," I wrote. "I have blamed you for what I couldn't see. I found fault with Leopoldville because I couldn't understand what this place could offer me. I want you to know that I'm still not sure, but I have now seen the variety and opportunity the Congo has to offer. Even in its most horrible moments, like the leper colony on the Kasai we stopped at this morning, I see opportunities. Opportunities to live, opportunities to enjoy a life here, opportunities to help the many who need it so much. I have never thanked you for bringing me here, Uncle, because I thought your motives were selfish. But I am thanking you now, Uncle Nissim. And if your motives were selfish, then thank you for that, too. I would never have seen this amazing world of yours if you had not insisted I come. I intend to do my best to make it mine."

AFTERWORD

LAURA VARON lived in the Belgian Congo for more than eleven years after her arrival there in October 1949. She married a few years later, and her first daughter, Clara, was born in July 1952. Together with her husband, Laura ran a general merchandise store and grocery that catered to both whites and blacks.

As the political situation in the Belgian Congo grew more and more unstable, Laura became increasingly concerned about the safety of her family. A student organization affiliated with Patrice Lumumba, whom Laura recalls as a tall and pleasant man with a deep voice, presented her with a gun, which she keeps to this day, and taught her how to use it. After numerous difficulties, Albert Kalongi offered the family use of a helicopter. Laura's husband took Clara to relative safety in Elizabethville and returned for Laura one month later as the revolution was already raging. When they were presented with the possibility of emigration to the United States, Israel, or Italy, the family chose the United States. They were among the first in the new Republic of Zaire to take advantage of President Eisenhower's offer of one hundred visas for former Congolese nationals.

On January 18, 1961, the travelers arrived in New York, and, with the assistance of the Jewish organization HIAS, they quickly set out for their intended destination, Seattle. Although she had lost nearly everything for the second time in her life, Laura was determined to build a new life. The family bought a little house, and in March 1962 a second daughter, Renée, was born in a local hospital.

Laura made a brief attempt to build a successful business from a small grocery in a dangerous area of town, but she quickly concluded that it was not the kind of life she sought. Unfortunately, her marriage broke up in 1968.

Her experiences during the Holocaust were something that Laura had never been willing to discuss publicly, but the situation changed in 1988. Now working in a local Greek restaurant and with people in a nursing home, Laura began to feel better about herself. When the University of Washington requested that she submit testimony to their Oral History Project to document the Holocaust, Laura agreed. This testimony was known as Laura's story. In 1992 she began to speak of her experiences to students at area junior and senior high schools. The warm response from the students and teachers have encouraged her to continue to spread her message.

In 1993, Laura Varon visited the National Holocaust Museum in Washington, D.C. She spent more than a week absorbing everything in the various exhibits. She was dismayed, however, to discover that the islands of Rhodes, Kos, Corfu, and Crete were missing from a map that displayed the areas of Europe that had been scarred forever by the Nazis. Laura drew the attention of the museum curators to this oversight and received a letter promising to correct the omission.

Although Laura has traveled to Italy and Israel, she has never gone back to Rhodes, and she insists that she will never return there. It is said that of the two thousand members of the Juderia in Rhodes, 104 survived the camps; however, Laura is skeptical that even that many made it through alive. She is determined that the world should know and remember their fate.

I've not been back to Rhodes since that day. I fear too much I would hear the whispers of my people in its streets. I fear too much I would stand before our house and see my mother at the door admiring the heavy purses of her Purim-costumed children. But most of all, I've not returned because there is nothing left to return to. There is only the shell of what was. There is only now a foreign place, like so many other foreign places I've been.

But I wonder if the Amora tree still stands and if it still shades young boys and girls, full of today's worries, dreams, and hopes. I wonder if fathers still tell stories to their children there and if the gypsies still visit in the summer. I don't know that I'll ever have the courage to find out.

About the Author

LAURA VARON, a native of Rhodes, survived the horrors of the concentration camps and vowed to keep alive the history and the memory of the Jews of *la Juderia*, a scant hundred of which lived through the war. After recuperating in Sweden, Laura eventually settled in the Congo. Years later she immigrated to the United States. She is a frequent lecturer on the Holocaust at schools in the Seattle–Tacoma area. This is her first book.